BOOM BOOM BOOM

The Rhythm of English Basketball

editor

Ian Whittell

YORKSHIRE ART CIRCUS

1997

Published by Yorkshire Art Circus   , School Lane,
Glasshoughton, Castleford, West Yorkshire, WF10 4QH.
Tel:01977 550401 Fax: 01977 512819 e-mail admin@artcircus.demon.co.uk

Editor: Ian Whittell

© Cover and book design: Paul Miller, ergo design

Production: Clare Conlon, Ian Daley, Jo Henderson, Lorna Hey

© Photographs

Peter Norton pages	6,13,16,24,29,33,36,37,44,53,61,63,65,68,72,73,81,85,87,90,91,
	94,97,100,103,105,108,109,115,121,123,131
James Brown pages	5,8,11,17,20,21,23,47,49,56,78,79,111,114,126,127,130
Ian Spooner pages	41,45,57,118,120

Printed by FM Repro, Roberttown,Liversedge

ISBN: 1 898311 35 8

Classification: Sports

We are grateful for support from Steve Catton and the EBBA and Probe Sports

Thanks to the teams and everyone who gave up their time in the course of compiling this book.

British Library Cataloguing in Publication Data.
A catalogue record for this book is available from the British Library.

Yorkshire Art Circus is a unique book publisher. We work to increase access to writing and publishing and
to develop new models of practice for arts in the community. Please write to us for details of our full
programme of workshops and our current book list.

Yorkshire Art Circus Web Site: www.artcircus.demon.co.uk

Yorkshire Art Circus is supported by

contents

contributors...

David Adams
Vickie Alder
John Amaechi
Tom Baker
Claude Bandawe
Liesel Bendel
Michelle Binder
Lisa Bird
Roy Blake
Paul Blakeley
Julie Boden
Paul Boden
David Bostock
Anne Bowyer
John Brady
Jim Brandon
Michael Brown
Steve Bucknall
Mike Burton
Kevin Cadle
Todd Cauthorn
Steve Catton
Magda Cetta
Darren Claire
Lisa Clarke
Leon Cockshutt
Betty Codona
Danny Coletrup
Liz Collins
Sarah Collins
Dave Coughlan
Sam Crosthwaite
Alan Cunningham
Peter Deppisch

Bob Donewald jnr
Sarah Dowling
Frankie Edwards
Jamie Edwards
Paulette English
Fiona Firth
Fab Flournoy
Emily Ford
Kevin Framp
Ian France
Dave Gardner
Martin Gibbs
Catherine Godolphin
Jay Goldberg
Panji Grainger
Paul Greaves
Ian Hall
Mark Hannen
Penny Hardaway
Roger Harrison
Pat Hawkins
Matt Hogarth
Colin Irish
Merrisa Jawando
Emma Jones
Matt Johnson
Jeff Jones
Kasey Keller
Pete Kelly
Matt Lawton
Barry Lea
Ricardo Leonard
Danny Lewis
Kate Lewis

Lee Longthorne
Kate McCormick
Ronald MacIntosh
Dean McDonagh
Steve McKenna
Barrie Marshall
Yuri Matischen
Janet Matthews
Fred Matthews
Mary Matthews
Robert Monaghan
Warren Moore
Stephen Moran
Natalie Morrissey
Dwayne Morton
Rebecca Nairne
Martin Nash
Ashley Nelson
Laszlo Nemeth
Jennifer Nurse
Nick Nurse
Deborah O'Connor
Steve Ogunjimi
Nigel Palmer
Michael Perfect
Ian Pollard
Craig Porter
Sally Potter
Kerry Potts
Ryan Pritchard
Peter Reynolds
Alan Richardson
Mark Robinson
Helen Rocca

Dave Rogerson
Katie Rolfe
Edna Ross
Neil Ross
Daniel Routledge
Kevin Routledge
Russ Saunders
Hilliary Scott
Katie Shooter
Robert Simms
Billy Singleton
Kevin StKitts
Matthew Smith
Mike Smith
Richard Stokes
AJ Summerfield
Neil Sykes-Hayes
Colin Tattum
Andrew Taylor
Dave Taylor
Janice Taylor
Mark Taylor
Louis Thomas
Paul Turner
Bruce Unwin
Matthew Ward
Andy Webb
Rob Webb
Joe Whelton
Melanie Woodhouse
Chris Wright
Harry Wrublewski

4

Foreword

Everybody needs something to inspire their body and their minds, something that makes every day battles worth winning, overwhelming odds worth fighting and everybody worth something.

For years in the United States, and now all around the world, basketball has been a way for young people to get ahead. A stepping stone to a free education, successful business and political careers, and in some cases, unimaginable fortune and fame, for those who otherwise might never have had an opportunity.

My introduction to the sport came with a couple of complete strangers coming up to me in the Arndale Centre, Manchester, and asking if I wanted to play basketball. One of those pivotal moments that parents always talk about, when a small opportunity, if taken, reshapes the whole focus of a person's life.

And although basketball has taken me across the world and kept me away from my family and friends, England and Stockport have never stopped being my home. It's where I first got interested in basketball and where the door to a whole new world of possibilities creaked open and allowed me to sneak out.

What I have achieved, and more importantly, who I have become, is thanks to a few select people in basketball in England - in the north of England - who believed in me, despite the ravings of those who said it could never be done.

In the beginning, basketball was a distraction, from a school that I found discouraging and the game of rugby which I found unfulfilling. But soon after I started, I found myself feeling like I had found my element - like a fish, stranded for so long on the beach, finally making its way back to the sea.

Basketball took my spirit and raised it to a whole new level. This wasn't because I was good - my first year I averaged less than a point and shot 26% from the foul line - but it just didn't matter, basketball brought me pure, unmatched joy.

My mother told me that everyone needs something that inspires their mind and body, some find this through study, others through vocation and others through sports. Basketball pushed the buttons in me that turned on parts of me that had never been used before.

Basketball is a game with very few natural restrictions, it can be played by almost anyone of any age and with varying levels of ability and mobility. It is fast, exciting and simple to learn. Basketball in Britain, at any level of skill, is an excellent vehicle with which to teach our children the ethic of success. A sport, where I have found even failure to reach the pinnacle of achievement within it, still leaves a person with valuable instruction that will have made them a more complete person. And I believe that at this time, any alternative means that will carry our youth towards fulfilment can only be a good thing.

Basketball has not made me a success and I won't suggest that it will do that for anyone else. However, it shone a light on my life that allowed me to view myself and my future in a whole different way. Finally allowing me to set new goals, gain a whole new focus and attack life with a new vigour. It is these things that make 'hoops' so special and valuable, and why I would hope to see basketball grow in Britain today.

John Amaechi

7

8

Introduction

Basketball is a complex dance that requires shifting from one objective to another at lightening speed. To excel, you need to act with a clear mind and be totally focused on what everyone on the floor is doing. Some athletes describe this quality of mind as 'cocoon of concentration'. But that implies shutting out the world when what you really need to do is become more acutely aware of what's happening right now, this very moment.

The secret is not thinking. That doesn't mean being stupid; it means quieting the endless jabbering of thoughts so that your body can do instinctively what it's been trained to do without the mind getting in the way. All of us have had flashes of this sense of oneness - making love, creating a work of art - when we're completely immersed in the moment, inseparable from what we're doing. This kind of experience happens all the time on the basketball floor, that's why the game is so intoxicating.

Phil Jackson, Chicago Bulls' coach (Sacred Hoops)

March 1995 found me in New York and, by a fortunate twist of the sporting calendar, led me to Madison Square Garden where the hometown Knicks were playing the Chicago Bulls and Michael Jordan, whom they had welcomed back from his self-imposed 17 month retirement just four games earlier.

The furore that greeted his return to the media capital of the western world was almost unprecedented and, like the genius he is, Jordan did not disappoint.

With his characteristic and heightened sense of occasion, Jordan turned in a virtuoso performance that, even by his extraordinary and almost unprecedented standards, was, to put it mildly, staggering.

Jordan's own coach, the articulate Phil Jackson, superbly sums up the breathtaking beauty of his - and other elite - players' talent in the above quotation. But, on this occasion, it was not simply the balletic quality and speed of Jordan's play that took the breath away. It was the sense that Jordan was toying with the opposition, scoring at will, no matter what combination of defenders and defences the Knicks - a team renowned for their defensive ability - threw at him.

This from a man who had spent the previous year and a half immersing himself in an unsuccessful career in minor league baseball.

To underline the point, as a close game reached its final seconds, Jordan had 55 points and the ball in his hands. Not unreasonably, New York's defenders lurched en masse towards Jordan who, with an exquisite pass, found an unmarked team mate under the basket for the winning shot.

It was a performance of rare beauty, one I still keep in the video library and which I have known to enthral even the most committed non-basketball fan. If you need to convert a basketball philistine in a couple of hours, may I direct you to the same tape.

The name of Michael Jordan features repeatedly throughout this book, the number of young people who quote him as their inspiration to take up the sport never ceases to amaze me. His shoe company were onto something when they coined the advertising slogan 'Be Like Mike.' His influence on the sporting landscape, from South Dakota to South Yorkshire and way beyond, cannot be understated.

But, of course, this book is about people whose talent - basketball talent, at least - is far more modest.

It is about people, of both sexes, all ages and cultures, who have contributed to making basketball, arguably, the fastest-growing sport in the world today.

You can find research that tells you it lags behind only football as the favourite sport among Britain's youth. And while research, like statistics, can tell you whatever you want, the voices in this book - particularly the young ones - suggest such a claim is not misplaced.

Other voices will express a conclusion to which my own experiences have brought me. Namely, that the coming two or three years are integral to the professional game in Britain.

Basketball has attracted wealthy entrepreneurs into ownership. Men who have been wildly successful in their own business world and have become hooked on the sport in the same manner as every other contributor to this book. Issues such as salary cap restrictions and the number of Americans teams should be allowed are pivotal to the development of the game and are debated, by far more learned and articulate people than me, elsewhere in the book.

What even the game's biggest critics cannot deny is that the sport, at a grass roots level, will not perish through lack of enthusiasm.

The North and Midlands of England - the cities of Newcastle, Liverpool, Chester, Leeds and, in particular, Manchester, Sheffield and Birmingham - are at the heart of this development, with lottery-funded outdoor courts springing up where tennis courts and five-a-side football pitches used to be. The development is a fitting metaphor for the spread of basketball itself, slowly taking over from other, more established, sports.

During many pleasurable hours of research for this book, I visited one such court in Rusholme, nestling in the giant shadow cast by a stand of Manchester City's football ground.

In one of the inner city's more neglected and under-invested areas, I was pleasantly surprised to see that not only was the outdoor court in full use, it was also in pristine condition. There was no hint of the vandalism or graffiti that cynics would expect to have already infected such a facility.

I asked one of its young users why this should be the case.

'Too many people use it,' he explained, almost bewildered by the question. 'We will all make sure nothing happens to it.'

A few months later I drove past the same court and discovered that the budding Michael Jordan, and his mates, had been true to their word.

That, above anything else, should tell you why basketball in England is so important today and why the voices in this book are worthy of your attention.

IAN WHITTELL

just do it

" a journey of a thousand miles starts with one breath . . . "

phil jackson

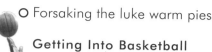

○ Forsaking the luke warm pies

Getting Into Basketball

🏀 To me basketball is something which has a rhythm. It has got the rhythm of the drum if you think about it - BOOM, BOOM, BOOM.

You are dancing. You can hear the music. That is the beat.

Then, when you have got somebody in front of you, you have to think of ways of beating that guy, trying to be deceptive. It is like dancing and grooving, that is what you are doing, it is similar. If you can't dance, you can't play basketball.

This American bloke, Adrian Dantley, used to play James Brown, soul music, before games and he said you have got to be able to do that to play basketball. I think that's true.

🏀 Watching basketball keeps you young. You don't need any tablets for stress, strain or tension because you can come and relieve it all on the refs! I've never had to go to the doctors suffering from nerves.

Everybody should have something where they can go and let off steam. We took one of my husband's bosses to an Eagles game the other night and she said, 'I don't know how you can stick this every week,' meaning the tension and excitement.

🏀 A lot of the emotion in basketball is generated by the proximity of everybody. Everybody is right on top of each other. In rugby or football, the coach or manager is up in the stands, he's no direct effect on the game other than talking to his team at half-time or at the end. In basketball, our coach is directly involved in everything that happens.

Every little emotion, every little mistake, every good thing, every bad thing, is blown out of proportion and everyone can see what is happening. That applies to the players, they get really emotional too. When a player dunks it, his team mates are right there, everybody is involved, everybody excited.

In football, in the build-up to a goal, three players might be involved and they might get really excited, the rest probably don't celebrate to that extent. In basketball, everybody is involved in everything that happens.

It is also a game of momentum, of ebbs and flows. Everything is intensified, everything is magnified.

🏀 We had this old-time 1940s radio at home, a big magnificent old thing, and we would crowd round, listening to the state high school tournaments, which are a big deal in that part of the States.

I remember going to see games at the high school gym, which was always packed, and it was just so exciting. It was like 'yeh!' I liked football and baseball but there was just something about basketball that hooked me. Just going out to play the game, something about the emotion of it, the sheer excitement. More than any other sport in the world. The other sports I loved, but you have to have a real passion for basketball.

As a kid, there was something about the feel of a basketball in your hand, shooting it for hours. Now, I'm running my own club, and that's as close as I'm ever going to get to playing the game professionally.

🏀 I think we've always been very traditional in the games we play in this country but that is something the kids are now very much moving away from. Why? I think it's because kids today are influenced by what they see on TV and by image. How does the image of cricket, for example, apply to a teenager today? It doesn't and that's why cricket is struggling in this country and basketball isn't. But

Traditional Games UK.

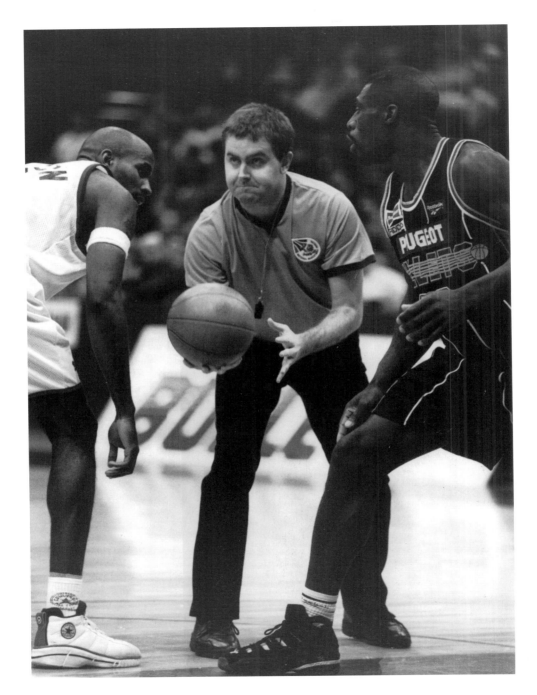

show a kid the NBA or roller-blading and the gear and everything that goes with it, the American influence, and they are hooked. Basketball is becoming their sporting heritage.

I discovered the game at college then went on to teach, where I did the traditional sports, netball and hockey, with the girls. I thought they'd quite like basketball so I let them have a go, they loved it and demanded more.

This was about 1961, at my school Hatfield, and from that the Sheffield Hatters were started. At the time, there was no other team in the country. We were the first women's basketball team in England.

I started it up because when the first lot of girls left school at 16, about eight or nine of them wanted to keep playing and we started the team as a sort of night school situation. They had teams in Scotland then, it was just that we were behind them, I think because we were probably immersed in the netball syndrome, very traditional.

🏀 He was only the size of a pea at the end of last season, we wanted to start him young. By the time he was melon-sized and into his second season, he was more than making his presence felt. It was either indigestion from all the pop and frozen yoghurt or the excitement and nervous anticipation that kept him awake and active throughout games.

When he was basketball size, I could hardly waddle down to the courtside. More kicking and booting, more yoghurt and pop. I feared the excitement would bring him on early and prayed for no more home games. I did, however, sleep soundly afterward, when he had exhausted both me and himself out.

At last, he was here in body and, at two weeks old, saw his first live game. He slept like a baby. I was so tired I couldn't concentrate.

At two months, he was awake and alert. The first quarter, he looked at the lights in the roof. The second, at the cameraman's glasses. The third, he spent in the St John's Ambulance room being fed

and the final quarter trying to sleep again. In between this frenzied activity, he glanced vaguely in the direction of the court.

I wonder what he thinks when he looks a long, long way up into the eyes of players peering down at him. I wonder whether he recognises the noises of the game, the cheering of the crowd, the echoes of the clapping, the cheerleaders' music and the squeak of rubber on court. Does he remember from before?

Next season, he'll have grown into his Jordan vest, he'll have yoghurt of his own and may actually watch the game.

His dad wants him to play basketball when he grows up and is encouraging left-handed rattle holding. Left-handed players are highly sought after, or so he says.

🏀 I've been playing basketball since I was born - almost literally! I used to get my nappies changed at basketball games, my mum used to have to call a substitution so she could leave the game and change my sister's nappies.

Mum and dad were fanatical players, at a pretty good standard, and there was just no way I wasn't going to be involved in the sport. Like most people in this country are with football, I was with basketball and by the age of seven or eight I was going down to watch the Riders.

🏀 Where I grew up as a kid, the neighbourhood had a basketball hoop, a little park at the end of the street which had a court and, although I played all three American sports, I really fell in love with basketball and committed myself to it totally at the age of ten or eleven.

That meant every single day of the year I would be out there playing, we'd be shovelling snow off the court so that we could keep playing year-round, and during the summer months we'd be at the court from nine in the morning 'til nine at night.

At my school you had to play a sport or a musical instrument during your lunchtime. Well, I played football for some time, in goal because of my size. My dad had been a really good amateur player with Oswestry so he pushed me slightly towards football and, because I was tall and long, I got put in goal.

Eventually I was cut from the team and, by this time of course, all the decent instruments had gone. The trumpet, trombone, sax, drums, you name it, they'd gone. The bassoon and the tuba were all that were left so that's how I became a tuba player.

I played it for about three months, sitting at the back trying not to be noticed. I played the odd note once in a while, making a lot of mistakes and wrong notes. I tried hard but eventually decided it wasn't for me.

Luckily our headmaster was very interested in basketball and had started a lunchtime team. He told me to go along and see how I did. I would have been 12 at the time though I can't remember how tall I was. I remember going to England at the age of 13 or 14 and I was 6'1" then, so I must have been pretty tall when I started. I also remember my first pair of boots, Nikes, size 12. Mum thought they would last for ever, of course, but after a couple of months I needed another pair.

I was born with weak ankles, I had to wear callipers, so football and rugby were out, I couldn't tackle or be tackled. So I had to try other things, I played a lot of cricket and still do, and that's how I came across basketball.

That was back in '83, at Woolston High School where we had a pretty good team. So, having got to know the game at school, I started going to Spectrum Arena in Warrington where the Vikings played.

It's the sort of sport where you quickly get to know other people, local league refs and players, volunteer helpers, other fans, and before long I was helping out, taking tickets on the door, keeping fans away from players, all the odd jobs.

When the team moved to Manchester all the fans were up in arms. None of the fans moved with them, just me and a couple of other helpers. The rest disappeared which was a shame. My involvement grew from there really. A part-time job became a more or less full-time job and I ended up in charge of the money, the gate receipts , which fitted in with my training as an accountant.

My one regret is that I didn't begin playing the game earlier. I started at 18. I was 6'6" at the time and it was pretty much a case of someone looking at me and saying, you should be trying basketball. I was doing my 'A' levels at college with a guy who was in the county setup. I started messing around with him and progressed from there.

I was always pretty athletic, from other sports, but I didn't have a clue about basketball.. Looking back, I just wish I had started playing earlier, it is just so difficult to catch up once you get to the top level.

I started playing properly at 12, when I was 6'2". When I first started I had my picture in the paper with two kids the same age as me and they came up to my waist. That's the way it's always been, really, and now I'm 6'8".

It was a choice basically between that and rugby and, to be honest, I was a bit of a tart. Call me stupid but I didn't want to go out in the snow and rain and get my head kicked in. You still get your head kicked in basketball, but at least you're not freezing to death while it's going on.

When I first started my co-ordination was pretty much the same as it is now - garbage. By the time I got to 16 I had problems with my knees and ankles. Every month I'd sprain an ankle and one or two were quite serious, I'd end up with my ankle the size of a football. That was through a lack of

 16

17

basic co-ordination, falling over myself or putting my foot in the wrong place, like on top of someone else's.

You find that all big guys are the same at that age but the good ones get through that stage. Players, like Matt Wright, who were bigger and heavier than me probably had worse co-ordination. It's whether you have the athletic ability or not that determines how far you go, and I never really had it. It's also a question of how hard you work at it.

Take someone like John Amaechi. He started at the same time as me and he'll probably tell you, he was nowhere near me for some time. But he worked his wotsits off. A few years later he's earning a million in Greece, and I'm here in Manchester.

🏀 I come from Malawi which is where I started playing, in about '76, when we had the American Peace Corps in the country. During the breakdown of colonial rule, the British just threw everything down and walked out. The system fell to bits, some schools didn't even have teachers any more.

So the President got in touch with President Kennedy and made a plea for help so a lot of qualified, ex-college people, came over from the States as volunteers.

At first I didn't want to play basketball, I just watched. I had already seen it at the cinema, the film that really caught my attention was *The Tall Stranger*. When I remembered how the whole game had been played around him, I thought I would give it a go.

The coach gave me a chance to play and I was there only two weeks with the team when they went off on a tour of central Malawi and he told me I would be the centre player, because I had unseated the guy ahead of me. I was the main man.

I was only 15 but 6'2", big and strong and I started playing against army people, I was bruised

all over the place and had to work very hard.

I did my studies and was promised a scholarship to go to the States but at the time there was a backlash against the Americans. The Malawi people had liked the Americans, because they were different to the British. But the political system was one-party and dictatorial and the government tried to get the students to recognise that politics in Malawi was 100 per cent straight. They wouldn't and challenged the President to have a debate and the Chancellor of the Exchequer was kicked out in 24 hours.

That meant a backlash against the Americans, because they were associated with the President, the basketball programme wasn't supported any more and basketball in the country went down, together with the scholarships that were promised.

🏀 The Supersonics were my first love. My dad used to take me to watch them when I was a kid and I've followed them ever since. The Sonics were a very successful team in the late 70s, so when I wasn't at the games, I'd be at home following them on TV.

They've come good again in recent seasons and I caught them in the NBA Finals against Chicago last year. Unfortunately, the English football season runs at the same time as the NBA, so I'm only ever back home for the Finals.

I was about six or seven when I decided I wanted to be a professional athlete. I didn't know which sport, I just knew I wanted to be one. It was probably a straight choice between football and basketball in the end, but I didn't make up my mind until I was 14. That was when I started to make some national soccer teams and really that made my mind up for me.

My first ambition was to get a full scholarship to university and football was the best way to do that. But I played basketball at high school until the coach told me to choose one or the other. I chose football and he didn't take it too well.

Now I still watch all the hoops I can on TV and get along to watch my local team, the Riders, whenever I can. I've done a couple of publicity things with them and really enjoyed it. Once you're hooked ...

🏀 This has been my second season working on Sky TV's basketball production, before that I worked for the Sharks in the office, helping out with entertainment stuff when they moved to the arena. I ended up doing a bit of everything with them.

Like most schools these days, mine played basketball and that's where I was first exposed to the game. I preferred it to netball immediately which was not a popular decision - you know, girls are meant to prefer netball, aren't they?

Why basketball? It's fast, physical, it's moving, I just found it more exciting and that was enough for me. I now consider basketball my career, not TV. That came about because of my connection with the sport, not the other way around.

My experience, in Sheffield at least, is that the people involved in the sport are generally very exciting and excited. They have to be vibrant, energetic people to help push the sport into the public mind and interest. You've got to be that kind of person, I don't think basketball is the sort of sport you can watch passively. It involves and excites you at so many levels.

🏀 I'd always thought it wouldn't happen to me. Men who found themselves deserting partners of 30 years or more for something else, were disloyal, spineless creatures. Yet it has happened, to me, a partner of 35 years has been replaced in my affections. Is this just a middle-aged infatuation? I don't think so. It happened like this.

January '96, Deborah, my youngest daughter, came home with the Manchester Evening News showing a special ticket offer for the Manchester Giants. She asked me to go with her. She seemed so enthusiastic, I didn't want to disappoint her (I certainly didn't tell her what I thought about basketball - 'a jessies' game played by abnormally large black Americans',) and so we went and my betrayal began ...

I can remember every detail of that night, I suppose you can when you look back on important events. The Giants were playing Birmingham and, from the word go, I was hooked.

What was it about basketball that so instantly captivated me? The presentation was superb. The Nynex plunged into darkness as each Giant was introduced, under spotlight, the speed of the game - at first difficult to follow but, after a few games, eyes and mind adjust. The excitement of a slam dunk. The skill of a three-pointer. The nerve-tingling agony of over-time. The enthusiasm of the crowd. Everything about basketball just swept me away.

Now both daughters and I are season ticket holders, members of the 'G Force', the Giants supporters club. We go to away matches as well.

I find it easy now to talk about players being 'strong in the paint' going 'coast to coast' and 'draining treys'.

Now power forwards, point guards and centres are of more interest to me than full-backs and strikers.

I have forsaken watery oxo, lukewarm pies and freezing afternoons of goalless draws for what Mike Shaft would call 'simply the best game in town.' And that is my betrayal. After 35 years of fidelity with Manchester City, I have found, in middle age, a new love - basketball and the Manchester Giants.

As Mike would say - 'Oh Baby!'

○ A cheerleader for Christmas

Kids on Basketball

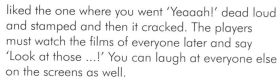

🕐 The best thing about the game was the cheerleaders, the blonde one. It was when they came out to dance, I watched her dancing. I'd seen cheerleaders before and I wish they'd sell pictures of them like they do the players ... I'd have bought one.

They get to plan dances to music, pick their favourite music and plan steps to it. It looks good when it's finished.

That dragon - I got his autograph. He was making a balloon thing and everyone was wanting autographs. He was good fun with all the kids, not just the little ones.

I liked the camera, we were all on camera dancing. It was great seeing us on camera. I thought we had ages to wait for the game but the camera and that Mega Man were there and you could sign and dance - and the cheerleaders. I'd go even if there was no basketball!

🕐 The guy, the player, who signed the autographs later, he was really tall and he signed four times for me, and so did Rocky the Cheerleader after the game. We caught him going home, I just said 'Sign the ball, sign the paper, sign this paper' and he did. Then he said 'Last one.'

I got loads of stickers and Peter got more but he swapped his with that bus driver.

These players are dead tall. I play basketball but I'm small. You can still be good but it helps if you're big. It doesn't matter if you're a girl. But these players were really tall. They've got to be so you can see them on the pitch playing.

I watched the replay on the big board because you could miss it when it happened in the game. I liked the one where you went 'Yeaaah!' dead loud and stamped and then it cracked. The players must watch the films of everyone later and say 'Look at those ...!' You can laugh at everyone else on the screens as well.

The game was cheap 'cos we got special tickets. I didn't have to pay with my money 'cos my auntie won on bingo. But Robert didn't have the money for a drink 'cos it was £1.10 - that's a rip-off - and Michelle had her drinks taken off her at the door.

All sorts of people play basketball. We only play it at school, there's nowhere like that place on Fresh Prince where you can play basketball, only at school.

The best trainers are Reebok, about £60 - they were wearing Reebok, the players, I think. The Cheerleaders were wearing free ones, I bet they get paid a lot and get all the clothes and trainers given them.

🕐 We all enjoyed going and liked the cheerleaders best. The players were good too but the cheerleaders were sexy and Mega Man, the mascot, was funny.

We liked it best when we had to shout 'Aaaaaaaah' and get louder and louder. We had some free cards, Robert got most but Peter nearly got his nicked. I wanted one of those shirts they had on but Mega Man wouldn't let me have it. They threw them out but I didn't get one.

The music stayed in your head later. The game was a bit boring at times because I didn't know much about how they played or about the players. If we talked to them and knew them it would be better.

They're supposed to be called the Giants - and they are! They're so tall, I could run between their legs. I want a cheerleader for Christmas. I'd like a cheerleader kit. I like the Giants outfit too, I'd buy one, but I'd rather take Rocky home.

24

O Jumble sales, rubber ducks and intimate liaisons

The Basketball Family

◐ We are one of several marriages who came together through basketball in the late seventies, early eighties. There must have been four or five of us married, just among the people I know. Not many of them go to the games any more, but basketball certainly brought them together.

We had a strong supporters' club in those days, running buses to all the games, and whenever we could we would tie it in with the football. If the football team was playing at Wolves in the afternoon we would drop the girls in the town to do some shopping while we went to the pub and the match. Then afterwards we'd be off to somewhere like Milton Keynes to watch the basketball.

Nowhere was too far for us. We had some real epic trips, going to watch the football team at Wolves then on to watch the basketball at Kingston. Or football at Notts County followed by basketball at Hemel Hempstead.

And when the basketball was at Eastleigh, in the days Solent were there, we would travel overnight. We'd have a lock-in at the Golden Lion at Houghton, then at midnight the bus would pick us up and we'd be off to the south coast.

Anyway, with overnight trips obviously overnight liaisons developed. People would be in drunken states and end up with other people, the usual lads' away trip stuff.

The thing with basketball, unlike most other sports, is that there is a big female contingent following it. I'm sorry but I still reckon that's just because of the attraction of the players. There's a big groupie element in the game.

In my case, the trip in question was a football match at Everton in 1980-81 - which we won 2-1,

coming from a goal down, Stan Cummins got one of the goals. We dropped the girls off in Manchester, went over to Liverpool for the football then went back to Manchester to see the basketball. I think we won the basketball as well. Drink took its toll, of course, and that was our first … what shall I say, intimate liaison. On the bus on the way back from Manchester.

◐ Basketball has made a big difference to my life. I came over here to university at Liverpool with a few people and one of them, Matt, played for the basketball team. I went to see Matt play and he introduced me to his team mate Paul, who later became my husband, so I owe my marriage to basketball.

We got married in April towards the end of the season and Paul had a game the next day! I don't remember who they played, but it was a home game in Manchester and that took the place of a honeymoon.

It was an informal wedding really, we were living in Leeds at the time so there weren't many players there and, in fact, we ended up getting married very quickly because I was going to end up getting deported!

◐ We can go back so many years with so many people and all the players are my boys. I never had a son, just two daughters, but I've had a basketball team to bring up for the past 22 years.

They all call me 'mother'. It can be a bit embarrassing when you walk into a room and a 6'10" black guy says 'Hi mom!'

◐ There's a big difference seeing Paul play for fun and seeing him play for the Giants. I don't like to see him playing for the Giants, last season especially. When he got out there he was, like, 'What do I do now?' He's just obviously not enjoying it so what is the point?

I used to watch him play for his college team

when he was THE star player and absolutely loving it. Now seeing him play for the last six seconds of the game, well, if it was me, I'd say don't even put me in. Perhaps that's why I don't have the discipline to be a player. I'd open my big mouth.

He has fun in pick-up games but I've never seen him look like he's having fun playing for the Giants. To me, it's a whole lot of commitment and a whole lot of abuse for something you don't appear to enjoy. What it is about Paul is that he's always played basketball and so he thinks he's got to do that. He thinks, this is what I've always done, so I'll continue to do it.

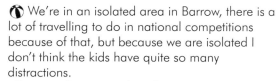 My mother always was, and still is, the inspiration in my life. She knew nothing about basketball but she sat down with me when I first decided to take it seriously and she was the one who supported my dream of playing in the NBA.

Sadly, she never saw me do it. But she got to watch me play at Penn State and we beat a nationally-ranked team at home on national TV - I had 19 points in the first half. She was always an inspiration.

I keep a photo of her in my wallet. It's a really American thing to do but I also think it's nice and I always think of her. Whenever times got tough in the States, whenever I had a bad day in practice or my arms hurt from lifting or I thought I had no chance of making it, I would just call her and she would inspire me.

Any time you have someone that important in your life you can never purge them from your memory, even if you wanted to.

My father left us when I was very young. I had contact with him once, while I was still in Stockport. I'm surprised I haven't heard from him since. I might recognise him if I saw him in the street but I wouldn't really want to. From what I know of him I wouldn't really care to meet him. I don't even know where he is … in the States I would imagine.

We're in an isolated area in Barrow, there is a lot of travelling to do in national competitions because of that, but because we are isolated I don't think the kids have quite so many distractions.

Being so far removed works against us in terms of the travel. Every match is a big away trip. Blackpool is our closest game, that's 80 miles away, Manchester is our next closest and that's 100 miles. We've lost four players from our cadet team this year alone because of that.

But being isolated works in our favour as well. It's not so easy for our kids to get out and about, go to big football matches or a big city, so they tend to focus on certain things - basketball being one of them.

There isn't a team where we can go in this country where there isn't somebody we know. That surprises a lot of people who are just coming into basketball now but we can go into any arena in the country and people who haven't been to a game for ages will come to the game just to see us.

In the old days we used to have a supporters' group and we used to get together and have a party after the game, win or lose.

But that was when basketball was enjoyable. There is too much money in it now, teams have got to win every week, there is too much pressure to win some trophy or other every season.

Fundraising is very important to a club like ours. The first time we did a jumble sale I couldn't believe it, we had people fighting over items. I once bent down to pick some clothes up from beneath a table and I got pinned against it and a wall. I had to crawl out from underneath it while people were fighting over clothing!

Then we've had duck derbies, when you release rubber ducks into a river or pool and the first one past a finishing line wins. We do it at Pond's Forge

now in the pool, but we've done them in rivers before and we've had to have people with nets trying to catch the ducks as they go past. I was once walking behind the 'race' wearing a pair of waders and suddenly the river bed gave way beneath me and I was suddenly out of my depth. I thought, here I am, about to drown because of a hundred rubber ducks.

🏀 I've got this bottle of champagne in the fridge that I've had for 13 years and I'm saving it for when we win something. I got it when we won the Founders Cup but never got around to drinking it, I think there was too much else to drink at that time.

So, we decided to keep it until we won something again. I don't think we expected that to take this long!

I've supported Derby since the beginning, since before they even went into the League. My sports teacher in school, a guy called John Bainbridge, was going to play so I went along. That was back in '81 when the team was run by Tim Rudge.

Derby is a pretty big basketball town, the sport has taken a real foothold there. I think one of the reasons is that when the team first evolved the football team weren't very good, they were in the third division I think, and the basketball was the ideal way for people to support something a bit more successful.

I've been through it all with Derby and that's why I would stick with them. I play myself, a women's team in the local Sherwood League, and they are my local team so even if I moved I would still support them.

I'm not changing teams until I see them win something .. and drink that champagne.

🏀 A lot of people call Sheffield the heart of British basketball, basically because of the long-term success the women's team has had and the immediate success that we had with the Sharks. All of a sudden we're the capital of British basketball.

What I have found is that while kids in Sheffield are interested in basketball, if you go out to the outlying areas - and we do clinics in Rotherham, Barnsley, Chesterfield, all the way in north Derbyshire, north Notts - the kids are even more into it.

It is part of the social spectrum, the kids all over are growing up with the sport.

🏀 We have a club philosophy that no-one will be excluded from our club because they haven't got money. So we have to do a lot of fundraising to cover expenses like booking refs and sports halls.

We have 60 per cent of our players from ethnic minorities, West Indian, Bengali, Somalian, Asian, the full spectrum. We take people from whatever background but they have got to conform, be out of trouble, stick to a structure and code on the court. We get kids from all over Sheffield and as far apart as York and Leeds.

The club was formed at Abbeydale Grange School, out of the National Schools winning team in '91. I was a teacher there, and now this is our fifth year as a club. We started as the Abbeydale Arrows but evolved into the Sheffield Arrows.

We run teams from ages 6-23, about 400 players, obviously all can't play for the team so we run sessions open to everybody. The better players we try to find competition for. Some go to regional leagues, Nottingham way, as there isn't any local league round us. And, those that can, eventually go on to play in the National Leagues.

There aren't that many coaches in the club - only about four adults - so we get some of the senior kids to attend coaching courses and ask them to put something back into the club. The qualified kids go and coach the kids at the bottom end.

There is quite a demand for basketball coaching right now, so we can fix them up with some sessions as well. If a teenager can earn £5-15 a week coaching basketball, it's better that he or she do that, rather than pot washing 'til one in the morning, if we're expecting them to play at the highest level.

Most of the coaching is free. They pay membership, this year it was £10 for the year, and match fees vary according to age. I think the under-19s pay £3 a match, but we would wave that in certain cases. We have kids travelling back from college to play, for example, so we wouldn't ask them to pay. And if a kid couldn't afford it, he wouldn't pay.

We've already had three players go through to the Budweiser League. Richard Windle and Mohammed Yusef with Sheffield and James Bamfield with Chester.

Mohammed was an Abbeydale pupil, I've coached him since he was 10. There's quite a strong Somalian community in Sheffield, and his was one of the first families to settle here. His dad was in charge of a bank but fled the civil war.

Mohammed is a naturalised English player now, I should know because I had to sort it out for him. He went to the European Championships with England when he was a junior. He was captain, but he got sent back because nobody had bothered to sort out his nationality. It was a major blow to him.

🏀 Sheffield is an amazing basketball city. I think one of the reasons is that it is a great city of sport anyway. There have been years of top quality women's basketball here and Betty Codona has been central to that. Sheffield Scorpions were in the first ever NBL Division One back in the 1970s and those people have stayed here also.

Wheelchair basketball then became established because of a spinal injury unit at Lodge Moor Hospital in Sheffield. It started with people in wheelchairs wanting to do something active and a team emanated from there.

The next big catalyst was the World Student Games being held in Sheffield, that's what brought me here from a job as general secretary of student sports in London, in 1988. They brought facilities and a focus on sport here and the next thing you know, that has energized all the local community to go out and get sports money in.

We then started a men's team in '91 to complement the Hatters women's team and the wheelchair teams that were already going. We got Pond's Forge and the rest is history - some good, some bad, but largely great.

You look at someone like John Belk, who played for Doncaster and England at the age of 19, who was the first ever player-coach of the Sheffield Forgers. He had stopped playing and came back and played and coached a year.

He's now coaching our under-14 junior Sharks and they've won a national tournament. He's coaching his son and daughter and now we're having to turn kids away at junior Sharks level. The Hatters are going to start a Division Two team, so there is a generation of new players coming through.

That's the good side of it. The bad side is that over the years we haven't been able to see eye to eye - the Sharks, the Steelers and the Hatters. Every day you try and work together but the difficult thing is we have had to establish a team on a professional basis and that means some of the things we have had to do have not concentrated on basketball development. We are questioned as to why we don't do more development work, but our players have touched 300 schools this season. We're going out there free of charge, and spreading the message.

29

○ Getting in your man's shorts

Basketball versus other sports

◗ Basketball has caught the imagination of youth today, it follows things that they see, exposure to things they see on TV. If you think about it, a lot of the programmes they see are about large, athletic people, even the game shows are like that. Look at the popularity of *Gladiators*. American football and WWF fall into that category, they're all about explosive athletes.

Rugby League had its resurgence since they cleaned it up, took it out of the mud and the muck, and turned it into a game of very big, explosive athletes.

Those sports that encapsulate those qualities are speeding forward whereas others, like cricket for example, which don't have that same explosive athleticism, are on a relative decline.

It's never one thing, of course, there are a combination of factors that bring changes about but that is certainly an area where I have noticed a change in emphasis.

Basketball in the '80s had a bit of a run on → 80's Channel 4 but died away. Now people have been fed the sport almost subconsciously, through adverts in cinemas, whatever.

◗ Basketball is a lot more involved than other sport. In football, for example, you might not see the ball for 80 minutes if you're a goalkeeper or defender and you're the dominant team on the attack. Similarly in cricket, you might be batting ten and fielding at fine leg and not do anything. If you're playing on the wing at rugby, you might touch the ball six times in a game, if you're lucky.

But basketball is played in such a small area with a shot clock that is forcing you to do something within 30 seconds, you are definitely a lot more involved and the game is a lot more dynamic than other sports.

If you are out there, there is nowhere to hide, you've got to be able to contribute and make something happen for your team, or at least not screw it up! Other sports can hide you if you have weaknesses, in basketball that can't happen.

The fact that basketball comes from America and has a tradition of trash talking makes it very emotional and very direct. There are so many one-on-one confrontations within that, I can only really compare it to boxing, nothing else comes close.

In tennis, you have the distance and you have the net in between you. Running also has that one-on-one competition, but without the physical contact. Nowhere else do you get that kind of proximity. Look at cricket, you have a bowler and batsman separated by 22 yards and when the teams do get together and get into verbal and nearly physical confrontations, it makes headline news.

You hear the expression in basketball, to get in your man's shorts - meaning to guard him closely. That sums up what I'm talking about.

◗ First and foremost, basketball is easy to play, but it is also fashionable. Yes, it's an American sport but I don't think that's its appeal pure and simple. It leads the way in terms of culture, its clothing, you can see why kids are sold on it.

The kids also have heroes there who I think they can live up to, they are tangible people. In cricket and rugby, the top players have traditionally come from a more privileged background. I know these are generalisations, but basketball players come from slightly less privileged circumstances.

What this means is the kids feel they can touch their heroes, aspire to do what they are doing and they can do that, not just on the court, but also by wearing the clothes and being part of a culture. You can't do that with cricket and rugby and I think the problem you have with football is just that

its stars have become untouchable. Look at someone like Alan Shearer, he is out of the average fan's league. He is almost an unreal, fictional character, he is so far removed from the kids' lives.

🏀 Basketball is my living now but with the hours I work, there is no way I could do it if I still didn't feel passionate about the game. A spectacular alley-oop still gets me out of my seat and shouting, even if I'm there working in a suit and tie.

The sport hasn't lost anything for me. On the contrary, I gain more from it now because I know more about what is going on and the people and personalities involved.

Even games that don't mean anything to me, I still enjoy. A few years ago I went to Filbert Street, Leicester City, on a freezing cold Boxing Day to watch a dull 0-0 draw when the first shot was made five minutes from the end. I wondered, why do people bother?

No matter how boring a basketball game may be, there is still usually something happening at some stage, some incident or match-up, or individual play that makes sitting through the game worthwhile.

The old saying about the game never being over 'til it's over has never been truer in any sport. The other week I saw Leicester trail Birmingham by 22, ten minutes later it's a two-point ball game. I've seen Leicester down six with 12 seconds to go and force over-time.

🏀 We've never won anything at Leicester, we've been particularly unsuccessful, so I turn my attentions these days to getting people involved, introducing them to the game. I play for a football team on a Saturday and get them to come to occasional games. I find if I can get people down to a couple of games they get themselves hooked.

I love the game, the whole shebang. It's very rare that you get a completely dull game, whereas in football and other sports you can get particularly boring games. In hoops, even if one team is getting walloped, it can still be entertaining. Stuff is still going on, there is plenty to watch and, if not, you can always have a go at the refs! Then there's the cheerleaders of course.

It is still exciting. The thing is, I didn't really play at school, so mine is not a playing interest, it's a watching interest. People believe the sport is mainly a participation sport in this country, but there are a lot of people for whom it is also a major spectator sport.

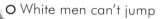

○ White men can't jump

Playing The Game

☎ The usual crowd had gathered for another hour of what we like to think is fast, furious and at times skilful activity on the basketball court.

We meet twice a week, come from varying walks of life, don't tend to mix away from the gym, but love playing the game.

Some of us are unemployed, some of us are self-employed, and some of us risk the wrath of our bosses by running well over the customary hour allowed for lunch.

It seemed like any normal Monday or Wednesday. Stan, a short, fat middle-aged man who sweats like a pig in a sauna and has an irritating talent for scoring three-pointers despite an appalling shooting action, was there. He volunteered, as always, to go skins, which is fine if you don't mind playing defence against a five-foot sponge.

Bill, a coach who has a voice like a distressed hippo, was there too and on my side, which meant endless on-court lectures on what my team mates and I were doing. There were plenty of lectures.

But it nevertheless appeared that we had the right people for two well-matched teams. Until that is, HE walked in. It just wasn't the height of the man that amazed us, although 6'10" gave him a considerable advantage, but the sheer size of him. We were later informed by a regular member of the group who had invited him along that he tips the scales at 20 stone.

He decided to join Stan and the bare-chested opposition for what was going to be an interesting 60 minutes. I sort of knew what to expect because I had been informed that he had spent last season playing in the NBA for Cleveland and was currently based in Greece, which boasts Europe's leading league.

But nothing could prepare us for the reality of actually playing against him. The speed which the ball left his hands to make a simple pass was frightening. It was like shot leaving a catapult and we were left wondering how nobody suffered a broken finger.

His speed of mind was just as impressive. His brain works faster than a Pentium Processor and he made his inspired colleagues look something approaching accomplished players by involving them in moves normally too sophisticated for our lunchtime sessions.

Yet it was obvious he was just having a bit of fun, and kindly doing his best not to flatten everybody. Bill, much to the annoyance of his team mates, moaned every time we stepped out of his way as he strolled effortlessly up the court. We told Bill to try it himself, and in his pathetic response he highlighted his advancing years.

But then who wanted to stop him? Even though we were being slaughtered, it was a joy to watch the great man in action. The school class members who often complain that we've run over time were applauding his every move, and he responded with a spectacular slam-dunk.

We came off the court thrashed but exhilarated and as we headed for the showers one of the younger lads discreetly asked who he was. That, I told him, was John Amaechi.

☎ Alton Byrd once gave me the best bit of basketball advice I think I got. We had just lost a championship game with Manchester United against the Birmingham Bullets at Stretford Leisure Centre, lost by three I think. I was 16, the youngest player on the team, and crying up against a wall.

I felt a hand on my shoulder and it was Alton. 'Don't worry,' he said. 'You'll be back next year, and people won't remember this. They only remember your last performance.'

That taught me. It was not only what Alton said, but also the fact that wherever you are, whatever you're doing, there's always someone watching.

🏀 I never saw much time in the National League, I probably only started one game for the Giants, at Worthing I think it was. I was the sort of guy who came on for the last two minutes of the game, the garbage time, when the game had already been won or lost.

That was what kind of annoyed me because I thought - no, I knew - that given the opportunity I could probably do better. But at 16 it's a big jump to go from junior to senior basketball and I don't think I could cope with it.

At that age I probably didn't have the physical ability either, I couldn't compete with the bigger guys like Trevor Gordon and Martin Henlan who would kick the hell out of me. That was off-putting. If you're only a kid getting the stuffing kicked out of you by a big bloke can really put you off the game.

🏀 I played one game for my dad's team, the Riders. I sat on the bench at Altrincham against Manchester. It was the year we went to the Final and we should have blown them out but we were short of players when we arrived and I was the only junior registered to play for the senior team - they had done that at the start of the season just to make up the numbers.

So I walked into the changing room and the guys were saying 'What are you doing in here?' And I answered, cool as I could, 'I'm playing!'

Karl Brown was on the team at the time and he was laughing and saying that if his dad owned the team he'd make sure he was on the team as well. And Dip, the coach, said that when his kids were old enough he'd have them in the starting five.

It was a game we should have won easily but we only won by five so I never got on ... but boy did I look good in the warm-up!

On the strength of that, I formed the 'One-game Club' for players who played one game but never actually got on court. My mate Mark Flanagan was a member for a while but he ruined it when he got on against Manchester.

I think I'm the only member now although I probably don't even belong, having made one appearance in a pre-season game for the senior side one year. It was in the summer, before the Americans had arrived, so I was there to make up the numbers and we got annihilated by a strong local league team.

I was desperate not to end up with a row of zeroes next to my name on the scoresheet so near the end I hacked somebody really hard to make sure I got on the scoresheet, even if it was only for a foul.

🏀 Until a couple of months ago I had pictures of me playing for England juniors on my wall but I got fed up of people turning round and saying, 'You were never good enough to play for England.' I've got pictures of me with Doctor J. When he did a camp at Stretford and I was picked to be one of the kids he coached.

Looking back, I don't think I realised what I had when I was 15 or 16 and I was one of the top ten players in the country. Every year there were trials at Lilleshall with 40 or 50 kids trying out, all of them after the one spot you had. At that time you don't think about what an achievement that is, or about what it means to all the other kids who you beat to that spot. I suppose it's something I should be proud of now.

🏀 People might not appreciate the advantage you get from playing and practising regularly on your own court. Not so much in terms of the support you get, but more than anything, the knowledge of how the rims play. A 15 foot jumper at one arena is going to rim out differently to another arena.

We don't practice at our own arena which is a

distinct disadvantage, so every home game I show up an hour early just to get some shooting practice in and familiarise myself with the rims, backboards and lighting in there.

That's also why the first thing I do, whenever I go into an arena, is take a few shots close in to see what the boards are like. At somewhere like Derby, where the boards are soft, you could throw up a brick and it would fall. Here, the boards are harder so you have to take that into account.

🕐 The slam dunk is the ultimate statement. A three point shot is worth three, one more than a dunk, but a dunk is even better than a three, especially when there is someone in the air trying to block you at the time.

I remember doing one against Doncaster. I was on the left-hand side of the court and the ball was in the corner with Kurt Samuels. He faked the three and I was running towards the basket hoping for the rebound. Instead of shooting, he hit me with a one bounce pass and I went up as someone came up to block it. Anyway I slammed it and it really is such a great feeling, all your team mates surround you, high five you. It's like 'Yeh!'

In a close game a dunk can be more valuable than a three-pointer because of the psychological message it sends to the opposition.

On the downside, it's the worst thing in the world if you miss a jam. You're the laughing stock. You're laughed out of the place! The whole place just stands up and laughs and that's happened to me as well. Last year against Hemel, when I went up for a two-hander.

As a player, the thing you have to remember is what you do in practice is kind of slow compared to a game situation. What you do in a game is always that little bit faster. In this case I ran so much faster that I mistimed the dunk completely and the ball bounced out.

Luckily, Joel Moore caught the rebound, faked it back to me and I was able to lay it up. So that

episode had a happy ending, although all the guys in the dressing room were teasing me afterwards - 'You see, white men can't jump.'

🕐 As a pro, you just want to put the ball in the basket, you don't really think about jamming it, you just think about finishing the play.
But ...
When you put it down on somebody, there is a big adrenaline rush, you feel great. Rising to the basket, hammering it on a defender, having some words afterwards to say to him. You just love it. You know that it puts a little fear in the defender and next time you go up he's thinking twice, 'Should I jump or should I let him get it by himself?'

I've never been dunked on in my life, I move out of the way to make sure it never happens. I'm not in the business of being dunked on.

But when a guy is dunked on, one of two things can happen. He can either be motivated to step his game up or disappear into a hole and not play for the rest of the game. You know, sign the poster of it when they come after you with it!

You either come back at them, or let them dunk on you again.

🕐 I know when I was growing up everybody still wanted to dunk but I wanted to work on my three-pointer. You get more three-point opportunities in a game than you do dunks.

Dunking is good but I think kids should be thinking about working on parts of their game they are going to be using more in games - you know, ball handling, passing, defence - and try and stay away from dunking it all the time. I'm not saying jamming the ball is bad - it's not - but kids should work on other aspects first.

🕐 Learning to play defence over here was tough for me because when I was in college I played tough defence. A lot of times over here that's

looked on as bad, they're going to call it right away and right away it means you can't control your man.

If I'm able to get up on him, making contact, then I can control him and that's how I've played defence all my life.

Once this year's over, hopefully I can come back next year and it will be totally different as far as my treatment by referees. You've got to earn their respect as a rookie. You're playing against a lot of guys who have been here for years and the refs are going to give them the calls.

I played against Kittles, Allen, Iverson in college - all guys who were taken high in the NBA draft - and held them to decent numbers. You know, guys who were averaging 30 would only get 12-15 against me.

So, defence is something I pride myself on, I was always known as a defensive player, a stopper. Hopefully, the more I play over here, the more I will understand the way the refs are and I'll be able to choose the spots where I can go up tight.

🏀 We lost heavily at Manchester, 82-46. It was just one of those nights when you had to hold your hands up and admit you had been taken to the cleaners.

At one point, late in the first half, you could already tell what we were in for when Kevin St Kitts got the ball just inside our half with two defenders on him and the shot clock ticking down.

Time ran out just as he shot the ball and it flew straight in ... swish! I just looked at the rest of our bench and rolled my eyes. When that happens, you know it is not going to be your night. You might as well get the engine running, get on the bus, and go home. That's exactly as it turned out.

🏀 We played at Tameside, a game which is always tough, there's always a bit of aggro when you go there. On this occasion, to make matters worse, the referees had failed to turn up so,

against some of our better judgement, we decided to play with one of their guys ref'ing.

Of course, it was brutal, absolute carnage and after the game - which we lost, surprise, surprise - there was still a bit of an atmosphere in the dressing room.

At Tameside, there is a beautiful swimming pool which you can see from the changing areas and it was a warm spring evening. We were sweating like nobody's business so, because the place looked deserted, me and my mate decided to sprint into the pool and cool off.

The only problem was we were stark naked and we had just swum one length of the pool when we turned round to see an over-50s women's swim group coming out of their changing room!

We had to swim the length of the pool naked and get out the other end to go back in the changing room. There were some expressions I'll never forget on those women's faces!

🏀 The last time Worthing won the championship at Wembley, three years ago, we had practice allocated for all the teams on the Saturday afternoon.

Sheffield came down looking ultra-professional, all wearing the same club gear and training very hard. Then it was supposed to be Worthing's turn.

It started off with a couple of kids, then I think Neil McElduff wandered in. Halfway through their hour, Colin Irish appeared. And that was it. No-one else from the team bothered to practice. Those four were just there, shooting around, playing around.

Then they came back later that night, Herman Harried was just amazing and made two massive dunks on somebody, and they won the semi-final. One night later, they beat Manchester in the Final.

🏀 Winning the Commonwealth gold medal with England in '83 was quite special. That was the first time I got picked for England, I was only 19. We

went to New Zealand, which was tremendous in itself, and ended up beating Canada in the Final. It was only their second team, because they also had a team in the Pan-American Games at the same time, but nevertheless it was still some achievement. It was a hell of a tournament to debut in.

On a club level, the season we won the league with Joe sticks in my mind, that was ridiculous. We started the season going 5-3 and we were ruled out of contention and, from there, we won 21 games straight and got to the point where we were playing Kingston in the second to last game and had to beat them by at least seven points, and win our final match, to finish ahead of them on the head-to-head.

Jeff Jones hit a three on the buzzer of that Kingston game and we won our last game by 12 to win the title. That was a great year.

(I played in the NCAAs in 1976 and hit a jump shot with three seconds to go against the University of Massachusetts to win the game by one. Then, the next day, we beat Providence who were ranked in the top ten in the country, we blew them out and I had, like, 25 points, eight assists, so I was MVP of the tournament.

Then we went on to Greensboro, North Carolina, and lost to the number one ranked team in the country, Rutgers University from New Jersey, in the quarter-finals of the NCAAs.

That was probably THE weekend of my basketball playing career. A whole life of playing basketball, of practising, all the dreams came true on that one weekend.

O Things like patella tendonitis

Injuries

(Sportsmen in general never make good patients, they're all a pain in the butt. They say never work with children and animals, well I'd add sportsmen to that list!

Basketball players are no different to others, they all have their own little ways and it's just a case of getting used to them. That's the challenge.

They're like footballers, they tend to moan about niggly little things rather than major issues. That's because they tend to get very few major injuries in those sports, compared to ice hockey and rugby league.

Those games are like working in a casualty ward. There are two types of injury - breaks and concussions. In ice hockey, we must get four dislocated shoulders a season, but injuries that serious are once in a blue moon in basketball.

Having said that, one of the worst injuries I've ever had to deal with in basketball was a seemingly trivial one that was really nasty. At the bottom of the tib and fib there's a ligament joint between the two. Mark Robinson had landed awkwardly and the heel bone had shoved up between the two and strained that joint. It meant that every time he put his weight on his foot, the foot got shoved up the middle of his leg. Very painful and a large bio-mechanical response for what sounds a small injury.

(It's real bad being on the sidelines injured, there's always that question of maybe you could have made a difference if you were out there. It's the not knowing that eats away at you all the time while you're trying to get fit again. Being out for a long time can be a messed up thing, you turn to

people you believe are friends and wonder if they really are.

I had two different injuries to the same hand in quick succession which made for a bad time and when you finally come back that can just be the start of your problems. Before, I played with a lot more reckless abandon, now maybe sub-consciously there will be that little bit of doubt in my mind, should I dive for this loose ball or will I hurt myself again? I suppose that doubt is only natural but you just have to get over that and get on with it.

⏱ We get an awful lot of sprained ankles, a lot of knee problems, things like patella tendonitis. An awful lot of them have got little problems with it and some of them do have traumatic knee injuries. It's because they work on flexed knees and the tendons are under strain all the time.

They suffer from bad back strain as well and that tends to be a result of having awful defensive posture. They don't flex their knees properly so they curve their back to compensate or, towards the end of games, the quads get tired and they can't sit back so much. You can't 'sit' on tired quads so as you get tired your legs straighten and to get to a lower position you have to bend your back.

⏱ We used to line up a set of stairs before we came out for games. I'd stand there and they would come past and throw these little balls into the crowd for the kids. Late one season, they were doing this and Kevin St Kitts threw one at me and it hit me on the head. Of course, the team did really well that night, so every game after that he would throw a ball on my head for good luck. It worked, we got all the way to the Play-off Final.

People wonder if, as a physio, you really care whether the team wins or not. I answer that if I didn't really care whether or not they won I wouldn't have let Kevin St Kitts throw a ball at my head week after week.

⏱ It depends what coach you're working with, but most accept your advice. When I was working with the last guy he would try and force me to allow guys to play who just weren't fit. That's why I left in the end, it was a case of, 'Why have you got me if you think you know everything?'

Now, with the current coach, I'm told if a player is not fit, he doesn't play. At the end of the day, I won't have the wool pulled over my eyes. That goes both ways. I've sent guys for MRI scans if I think a player is pulling a fast one, doesn't want to play for whatever reason. You see guys where the pain moves every two seconds, they don't know what's up with them.

And you can get into the sticky area of patient confidentiality where the player tells you something but doesn't want the coach to know, you have to tread carefully between what they want the coach to know and what you feel they need to know.

But, of course, it's not as simple as, 'Yes, he can play. No, he can't.' I will negotiate with a coach. I'll tell a coach he can have him for this game, but not the next, and ask him what he wants, or tell him he can only have the player for 20 minutes.

The last coach was the only person I've ever worked for who totally disrespected my opinion. It got to the stage where one of the players had a screaming match with him about it.

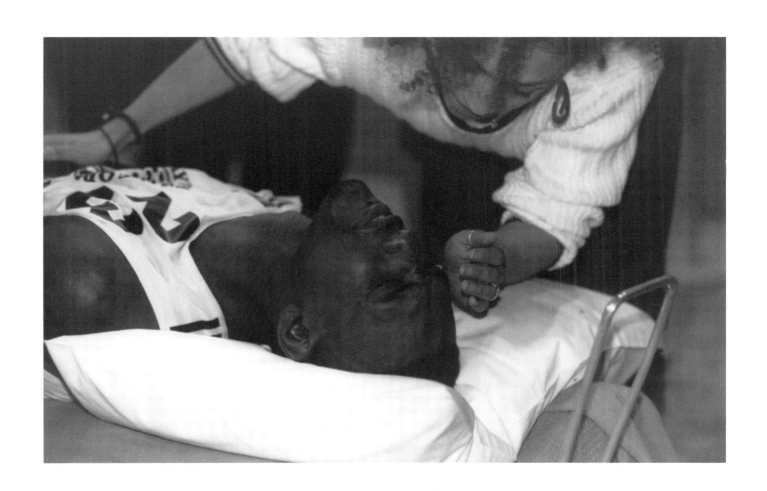

○ Everyone has a Trevor Gordon story

Talking Trash

For my money, Trevor Gordon is the toughest player I've seen, THE big man. Whether it was legal or not, Trevor wasn't scared to dish it out, especially in European games when the occasional elbow would fly.

Whereas the best some guys can do is to turn round, square up and start verbaling their opponent, Trevor wouldn't stand around and get his handbag out, he would have a go.

I remember Manchester playing a Spanish team, Estudiantes I think, at Altrincham and Trevor just turning around and flooring someone who had annoyed him with a swift elbow. The referee doesn't see a thing, the guy is rolling on the floor holding his face and Trevor is jogging down court with a big smile on his face! Brilliant!

Trevor wasn't scared about going up against anybody, whatever the game, whatever their size. He just wasn't bothered about it. And, as a team mate, you knew that if you got into a scrape he would be there for you. He wasn't called 'Big Daddy' for nothing.

When I was with the Giants we played the England representative team in a warm-up game and Trevor just threw me over his back. It wasn't intentional. I tried posting him up and he just rolled me straight over his back and threw me on the floor. I would have weighed, 16 and a half, 17 stone at the time and he just picked me up and threw me over.

The combination of playing against him and Martin Henlan made you feel like a rag doll being tossed around.

One time we played Guildford and one of our guys, Rick Lloyd, picked a fight with Trevor. Soon after we were at the free-throw line and Trevor and Rick were still growling at each other and Trevor said to Martin, 'I'll take this guy,' pointing at Rick.

Martin says back, 'And I'll take this guy,' pointing at me! That was it for me. I immediately called for a sub and turned round to see Trevor and Rick squaring up again and I'm shouting to Jeff , the coach, 'Get me out of here!'

Poor old Matt Wright had to go in for me and, sure enough, he got it instead, which was alright by me. People might say I bottled it in that situation but hey, my features aren't that great to start with, I don't need them making any worse.

I was playing for Chester one time against Guildford who had Trevor Gordon with them at the time. We went for a rebound and I boxed him out, caught him really hard, and next time down the court he swung at me, caught me on the head.

The ref saw it and kicked him out of the game for it. It was a good example of how you can make those situations work for you.

As a postscript, I have to say the good thing about Trevor was he would be cool after the game, even after a game like that. Years later, we went on to be team mates at Manchester and always got on really well.

But Trevor was just one of those players who was always very easy to upset. You found that if he didn't get the ball in the first few minutes and score then he would have a bad game. He needed to get going early.

He went over to Europe last season and I guess that is where he will stay because that is where the money is. But I'll tell you something, for all he has a bad reputation at a lot of places, particularly with management, there are probably at least ten Budweiser League teams who would take him tomorrow if he came back.

Everyone has at least one Trevor Gordon story. I remember him playing Hemel once and Trevor

taking a few of their guys out, Jody John had a go back at Trevor and it all got out of hand. It was such a rough game, even Paul Boden was fighting that day!

At the end of the game, Trevor just strolled off, thinking nothing about what had gone on - it was another day at the office to Trev - and back to the locker room.

They had a guy called Mike Carty playing for them who was about 6'4" and nearly as broad as Trevor is. He walked into the dressing room, on his own, pointed at Trevor and said, 'Gordon. Me and you outside now.'

Trevor looked genuinely amazed and then all the Manchester lads jumped up and surrounded him and Carty is screaming at Trevor to come outside, 'You think you've got such a big reputation, Gordon, knocking people out, well I'm going to knock you out!' It was bedlam. There were all these young kids outside in the corridor waiting for autographs and all this is spilling out of the dressing room door and almost out into where the kids were standing!

It's a shame they never got it on, the pair of them, it would have been an interesting fight. Full marks to Carty, though, for coming into the dressing room on his own. A brave man. Or stupid …

🏀 When I'm playing defence against someone and they're talking trash, to me it means I'm messing around with their head, rather than the other way around. They are being put off their game by concentrating on talking trash to me and I take that as a compliment.

For instance, if I box someone out and catch them hard with an elbow, they might come back with a threat like, 'Next time I'm going to take you out.' Well, that means I'm getting to them if they're thinking about knocking me out they are not thinking about their own game. It means I've got that guy.

I've had that a few times, if my man takes a swing at me then he's not thinking about his jump shot or rebound.

There was a guy who used to play at Hemel, a really nasty guy, a real tough dude. I can't remember his name but I wound him up every time he got the ball in one game. In the end he was so desperate to score on me, he would hurry his shot and miss.

He punched me as we were walking off court at the end of the game, caught me on the back of the head when I wasn't looking - real brave. In fact he still wasn't satisfied when we were up in the bar after the game. He started having a row with my wife. She said something to him, but not much.

🏀 I was never any good at trash talking, I just didn't bother with it, kept out of it. I tried to never react if someone had a pop at me. If you got too wound up, tried too hard to beat the guy, then that would just upset your game.

Carl Miller is superb at it. He's probably the one player who wound me up the most. I was 18 when I first played him, you know, the bench boy coming on for the last two minutes and he's asking questions like 'Why have you bothered coming?' 'What's the point of bringing this guy on?' 'Hey, the skinny white kid's on!'

🏀 We once played in an anti-apartheid tournament at Telford and first of all there was a fight on court and as Jeff Jones, our coach, went on court to try and sort it out these guys run on after him and smack him in the head with a can.

I think Jeff was concussed because five minutes later, in a time-out, he suddenly rubbed his head and asked, 'Who hit me?' He didn't even realise he'd been hit.

Late on, Roger Duhaney turned round to me - I'm a 16 year old kid at the time, remember - and said, 'Oy, white boy, what are you doing playing this game? Go back to playing hockey.'

43

○ Hunger. Desire. Courage.

The Players

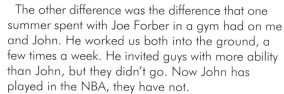

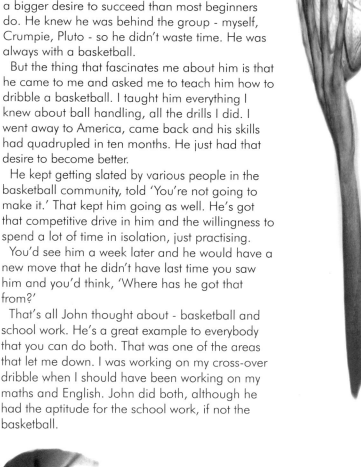

I always remember the first practice John ever came to. He couldn't dribble and walk in co-ordination. Throwing the ball at him was like throwing a plate of jelly at him. But then he was no different than any other beginner, apart from in a couple of things.

One, he was smart enough to realise the people around him knew better. Secondly, he knew he had a bigger desire to succeed than most beginners do. He knew he was behind the group - myself, Crumpie, Pluto - so he didn't waste time. He was always with a basketball.

But the thing that fascinates me about him is that he came to me and asked me to teach him how to dribble a basketball. I taught him everything I knew about ball handling, all the drills I did. I went away to America, came back and his skills had quadrupled in ten months. He just had that desire to become better.

He kept getting slated by various people in the basketball community, told 'You're not going to make it.' That kept him going as well. He's got that competitive drive in him and the willingness to spend a lot of time in isolation, just practising.

You'd see him a week later and he would have a new move that he didn't have last time you saw him and you'd think, 'Where has he got that from?'

That's all John thought about - basketball and school work. He's a great example to everybody that you can do both. That was one of the areas that let me down. I was working on my cross-over dribble when I should have been working on my maths and English. John did both, although he had the aptitude for the school work, if not the basketball.

The other difference was the difference that one summer spent with Joe Forber in a gym had on me and John. He worked us both into the ground, a few times a week. He invited guys with more ability than John, but they didn't go. Now John has played in the NBA, they have not.

Talent alone is not enough.

We're the type of team that over-achieves and a lot of times when you're that kind of team, you have the psyche of a boxer. That's the parallel I always use because boxing always brings out the innate aggression, confidence or lack of confidence. It is one of those sports where there is nowhere to hide, and basketball is like that.

When you're used to winning, winning, winning and somebody hits you with a good shot, or you get KO'd, it's not necessarily the same animal that comes back into the contest.

Personally I like to think I'm a warrior. Psychologically I'm fairly good at getting things across to people and I absolutely relish the situation of getting the team to respond.

When you separate the men from the boys, I know which side of the line I want my team on. That's the bottom line. You can talk all you want about tactics and the various options but when it comes down to it, it's the beast in you.

Vinny Jones may not be the greatest footballer in the world but he tends to get the job done. Evander Holyfield is not the most gifted boxer but he gets the job done. That's what it's about. Hunger. Desire. Courage.

It's a cliche but I think sports, and basketball, is a metaphor for life. In both, you go through the whole range of emotions on a daily or weekly basis. Somebody, like Roger Huggins, is going to be on a lot more of an even keel, because he is established. But for someone like me, who was coming on leaps and bounds, those emotions were magnified all the more.

50

I was trying to get somewhere, improving, you could see the development and when you sit and look back, it brings a good feeling to you. The joy you get from improvement, the sheer joys of winning, the lows of losing, you never experience that in any other walk of life. Sure, you may get praised for something you do at work but you don't find it as a rule in anything other than sports.

If you have any sense of emotion in work you tend to find them masked, you cannot mask that passion for sports, the passion for competition and the game.

You see guys, ordinarily level-headed guys, out there on the court, arguing, back-chatting, kicking chairs, even fighting. That's the passion of the game. It's irrational behaviour and you don't get it outside of the sporting environment.

🏀 Chemistry in a basketball team is so important. When there is good chemistry you make better decisions as a player and you know exactly what the other person is going to do, when and how.

If you don't have it on and off the court then that is a recipe for trouble. A lot of times bad chemistry starts off the court then ends up on it and that can effect games. You lose games you are supposed to win because guys are bitching with each other.

We have a great chemistry at Chester, a bunch of guys who are just happy to be playing with each other and are just happy to hang with each other off court. That shows in the results we have got this year. Considering Chester has been a bottom-placed team for so many years, even with four Americans, the results have shown a real dramatic change.

That usually doesn't happen overnight in sports but when a group works well together, when they have that chemistry, that is what can happen.

🏀 Joe Hillman is the best player we've had at the Giants. Will Brown was a nice player but could disappear in the big games and Rick Lloyd

became a good friend, so I'm biased there, but Hillman was the most effective player we've ever had.

He was a controversial bloke though. The saying went that he had more air miles that season we had him than points. He went back to the States so often he was practically commuting between Indiana and Manchester by the end.

I think he was here for the first 20 games and then he got worse as the season wore on. As his relationship with the coach got worse, Joe started finding business interests back home. Whether they were legitimate or not I don't know but twice I remember him flying into Manchester on a Friday, playing the game - and winning - on the Saturday and flying home straight away afterwards. It didn't matter to Joe and in those days the owners were throwing money at it so they didn't care either.

I think Joe just got sick of the way the club was run, the lack of discipline. What brought it to a head was a game with Chester when Trevor Gordon got kicked out of a game for picking up two technicals and Joe demanded that Trev be kicked off the team for it. The coach said no, and that's when all the problems started.

🏀 Terry Crosby - 'T.C.' - was the best I ever coached. A sensational player, very talented. I was coaching him towards the end but I also saw him in his heyday.

My most memorable Crosby game was actually one when he hardly scored a point. Terry was always noted for his big numbers, a big scoring player but one game I asked him to play a different role and play point guard. He only scored two or four points but he ran the game, dished out dozens of assists and we won the game. That told me a lot about T.C.

I had him for a season with Bury, my second season there and we finished mid-table. He was quick, had great skill, left or right, shot the ball, was physically very strong, 6'5", had great

anticipation. He knew how to put points on the board. Great crowd pleaser, people came from all over to watch T.C.

A great player, a great person, a very huge talent. It's a pity he isn't around now, he would easily have been as good as someone like John White at the Leopards.

He was the bee's knees, really had the gift of the gab as well. Last time I heard of him he was still up here in Bolton, selling space for advertising or something.

🏀 Pete Mullins was another of your legendary hard men. I remember us playing Ceserta from Italy in a European game at Stretford and a big fight kicked off after Jeff Jones threw the ball in an Italian's face after they scored.

There was one of those complete bench clearing jobs and everybody was up. Of course Pete got involved, never one to take a backward step, and he had this Italian in a headlock in front of their bench, and this guy could not breath.

They had those little wooden benches at Stretford and Pete and this guy had fallen straight over and were practically sitting in the crowd and this guy was still not breathing. I'm not sure who, but one of our players dragged Pete off this guy and the Italian couldn't move for about a minute. Another couple of minutes and it would have been lights out for the guy.

🏀 A few years ago we were desperate to get some big coverage in the nationals and a reporter came down from Manchester to Guildford to interview a guy who played for them called Tracey Pearson.

Now Tracey was a huge guy, he was about 6'9" and 22 stone, absolutely immense, and with a real temper to match. During this game he was murdering Derby and was close to getting 50 points. But the game was such a rout that Kevin Cadle brought him off when he was still a few points short.

This really ticked Tracey off and, after the game, the reporter went up to him to talk and Tracey just walked straight past, he wouldn't say anything. I thought, great, he's come all the way down the length of England for an interview and got nothing, this will set us back years! Fortunately, we got a great piece out of it, a full page in The Sun.

The piece included a great quote from Cadle who claimed someone once asked him for Tracey's stats and he replied: 15 Big Macs, 12 portions of fries, 10 cokes ....

🏀 Basketball players on court are entirely different people off the court. When they put on a uniform you can find the nicest, gentlest person turn into an animal. I think basketball players have a few brain cells missing. For one, they have no consideration of time. Time waits for them, not the other way around. If you want a ball player to be on time, then make sure you tell him to be there three-quarters of an hour before you want him. I've never found an exception to that rule.

🏀 Basketball players' private lives never cease to amaze - and amuse - me. My favourite, and very common, scenario is the one where a player asks me for four tickets for a game, I'll give him them and he immediately asks to exchange them because all four are seated together. He needs two in one section of the arena, two somewhere else to keep his female 'associates' separate.

I've had to pretend to be someone I'm not. An American player's long-term girlfriend came over from the States and wanted to know why another girl had answered his phone a week earlier. 'That was only Sue,' he said. Luckily, his girlfriend failed to notice that the 'other woman' was English, whereas I've got an American accent!

Then there was the time two guys were sharing a house. A woman came to the door for the guy who was out, so his room mate let her in and she went to the bedroom. Unbeknown to the guy who let her

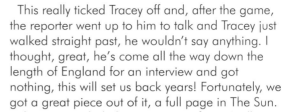

in, his mate was actually out on a reconciliation date with his wife. They were trying to save the marriage after a trial separation. The wife coming home to find the girl in the bedroom didn't help matters!

There is a certain calibre of players in this league who knows that just because he is a professional sportsman, certain girls will be attracted to him. I've seen one guy wear his team vest to a night club to try and look important, I've known a guy who will hit on a woman in a queue at an airport.

One England international, who better remain nameless, once hit me with the classic. 'Are you married?' 'Yes.' 'Are you happily married?'

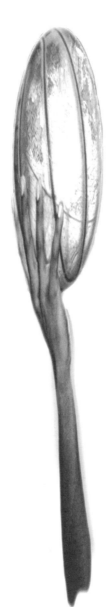

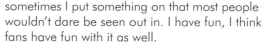 Bob got wind of the fact that one of his players Justin Phoenix had won the player of the month award, which is worth a crate of Bud to the winner, but the guys still hadn't heard by the end of practice.

So he called them all together, sat them down and told them what a great team they were and how important team work was and that any personal accolades that they won belonged to all of them.

He went around each of them individually and got them to agree to it and, as he was walking out, said 'Oh well, I guess the beers are on Justin!' He nicked the prize off him before he even knew he had won it.

I'm the one that gave Clyde Drexler the nickname 'Clyde the Glide,' during my time as sports information director at the University of Houston. The way it happened, Darrell Griffith was called 'Doctor Dunklestein' at the University of Louisville and my boss said, 'We've got to come up with something for us.'
I said, 'What about 'Clyde the Glide?'

I wear some wild clothes, no doubt about it. I like to dress sometimes plain, sometimes casual,

sometimes I put something on that most people wouldn't dare be seen out in. I have fun, I think fans have fun with it as well.

There are some other guys around the league - Jim Brandon, Kevin Cadle - I've seen those guys dress up. I just don't know if they get as flamboyant with it.

The one thing this season has taught me is that money is a necessary evil, no more, no less. You need it to survive, but there is a very big picture above and beyond money.

What brought it into perspective for me is that my mother-in-law is in a hospice with cancer and I've got a younger brother, Joel, who has contracted the AIDS virus and is fighting for his life. He's in the States and he's promised me he'll still be there when I go back there at the end of the season. Meanwhile, I'm watching this woman, my mother-in-law, fighting for her life and I'm just happy to wake up each day and be alive.

So many people have it worse off than me. So, I don't know how much longer I'll keep playing and it doesn't really matter. I just hope that Patricia lives a painless life for the rest of her life. I'm not even thinking about what I'm doing next year, I'm just thinking about what's happening today. It puts it all in perspective, doesn't it?

I was there the night Tony died, it's not a nice thing to talk about even all these years later. Looking back now, I can't forget the fact that Tony was on medication for his heart and had stopped taking it because he thought he was over the worst of whatever problem it was he had.

His heart was unstable and would just go haywire. I think after his death they found it was three times normal size.

Tony had started the game, I think Dave Gardner was injured, and wasn't playing particularly well. But typical Tony, he had given his all and he came off after eight minutes. He sat down in between

Dave and Chris King and I remember him gripping Chris' knee.

Tony leaned over and put his hand on Chris' knee and I remember Chris shrugging it off, slapping his hand away, sort of saying, 'Get off, what do you think you're doing!' Then Chris looked at his face and his eyes had gone, he had had the attack. Chris said later that Tony had gripped his knee so hard that it drew blood. I don't know if that's right but, whatever, Tony just keeled over and died.

I always said the Giants should have retired Tony Penny's number - number 12 - for all-time, as a mark of respect. But a few years later Yorick Williams wanted to wear it and I don't think there was anyone left at the club who remembered Tony, certainly nobody who felt strongly about it. That was wrong.

The days of teams training from seven until nine a couple of days a week are gone. I remember working all day, being on the road somewhere at six and having to drive like a maniac to make practice for seven. You arrive stressed and not in a good frame of mind, I couldn't still be doing that.

Two seasons ago we had a week day game against the London Leopards on an evening when there were horrendous snow storms. We got stuck in a drift on the motorway and got back at 6am! My wife works for the Giants so she just got in and went to sleep. I had a shower, a cup of coffee and went straight off to work. That was horrible.

It's very difficult to balance a full-time job with playing basketball at the top level. When both demand your time you have to definitely make a choice at some stage, you can't do each 50-50, you've got be 90-10 one way or another.

Last year my basketball came first, the job came second, it was very stressful purely because you have so little time. Other players get time to relax,

get mentally set, sleep in all day if that's what they need. With a 9-5 job, you go home from work, practice and just miss that time to yourself.

I was lucky in that I worked for the organisation so I was given time off for practice, but I've done the 9-5 thing as well and that's very restrictive, you end up taking all your holidays to play basketball. You don't have a proper holiday all year.

Once I decided to take a sick day when I was working in a building society in Leeds. We had practice that day and, inevitably, I got a black eye in a scrimmage. I had to go to work the next day with my wife's make-up covering the mark. Luckily they didn't notice.

But as the League develops, it is moving away from the part-time players. As the money gets bigger, the demands to win get greater. That means more practice and most teams practice during the day now. That's fine if you're an under-23 player, most of them tend still to be at college or living at home, but it's not so easy if you have to worry about mortgages or families.

You get used to the routine, doing weights in the morning five times a week. You hate it at the time, it's such hard work, but when you stop you almost miss it. That's the worst thing about getting cut from a team.

A few weeks after I was cut, I found myself going to practice once a week just to feed the urge, I was getting desperate to play. Your body and your mind get used to the conditioning and while you're tired by the time summer comes around, once the season starts again you realise how addictive it is and start looking for a substitute. Anything to stop me spending more time with the missus, I suppose!

You miss the peripheral stuff, the free stuff like gym membership. And the bottom line is it feels funny sat in the stands when you expect to be down there on court. You're just another spectator.

You also find a huge amount of little kids coming up to you and ask why you don't play anymore.

And there is no doubt that you miss the social side of the game, hanging around in the bar having a pint with other players after the game. It's alright now because they all still remember who I am, but in a few years, who knows?

It's just an ego thing, I know, but you really feel important when people want to talk to you. You're at the front, you're part of the show.

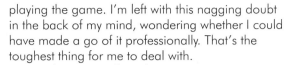 It's funny but since I left the team, I find it hard to sit and watch a game without having anything to do. I used to sit on the bench and hand out towels and other stuff to the players but I'd also do offensive stats and analysis. So now I can't watch a game without wondering how the team is doing against a 3-2 zone or how many passes we make or how long there is left on the clock when we take a shot. Unless it's a great game I find it difficult just to watch.

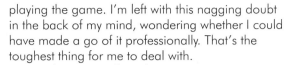 It's tough after you've stopped playing. Growing up, I had been involved in some kind of sport or other, that I had taken it for granted at the time. Once you are taken away from it, you definitely miss it.

It's that feeling of you and however many other guys - 10 or 15 - going through all the highs and lows of the season, what that brings. The sheer joy, the depths when you lose, the fact that you are sharing all that.

I find it very real being in a sports environment. When you do well, the guys are whooping and cheering you. If you fail, guys are in your face telling you about it, trying to make sure you don't do it again. Compared to that, I find the work environment very static, uptight in comparison. You don't have that emotional release you have when you are playing sports. I miss that stuff.

The difference is, from a competitive point of view, I'm left not knowing. There I was, 6'9", can run and jump real well, I know that I can play the game but because of circumstances, I'm not

playing the game. I'm left with this nagging doubt in the back of my mind, wondering whether I could have made a go of it professionally. That's the toughest thing for me to deal with.

I miss the camaraderie, knowing you can compete. It makes it difficult even to watch games now. Sure, I can watch the NBA, but watching guys who were my peers and who I played against, I cannot do.

I know the League has improved but I feel I could still do a job for some team at some level. But that would demand full-time commitment which is something I couldn't give while I'm working as well.

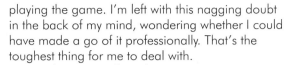 My daughters say I'm crazy. Believe me, that's what keeps me going, I think young. My mum and dad always thought young and I've inherited that from them. Mum is 64, Dad 68 and when I go home to see them, I don't know where they get the energy from. I'm only 42, but they put me to shame.

One of the biggest mistakes I've made in my career has been listening to people try to talk me into retirement. Perhaps it's a very British thing, but when you get to 30 years of age in sport people say you should be hanging your shoes up. Why? Am I not still doing the job?

When I break down and just can't do it any more and they have to carry me off the court because I'm hobbling so badly then I'll think about it, not before. I look at Ray Wilkins, who must be the second oldest professional sports player in the country after me, and I related to what he said after he left QPR as manager. He said he didn't want to manage, he just wanted to play. I'm the same, I just like playing. The competition keeps me young. I don't drink, I don't smoke. When you get to my age, basketball is the only vice you have left!

○ I'll give him a kick in the ass

The Coaches

Now I'm involved in the coaching side more, I realise what a kick in the backside a bad defeat and a poor performance can be for the organisation.

You get over 9,000 people in to watch a game and you get blown out by 20. As a player, you're down for a day or two but it's just another league game, another two points, that you have lost, the fact that it is harder for you to win the league.

But on the management side, when you have worked that hard to get the people there in the first place, then you are left wondering and worrying whether those people are going to want to come back. It can effect your financial predictions, your long-term goals, everything. It's about a lot more than two points.

Personally, my philosophy is about the pressure within. I'm a pretty intense guy, everyone knows that, whether people like that or not that's a part of my personality. I'll smile before the game but during the game I want to go for the jugular. From my point of view the biggest pressure I've ever dealt with in my entire life is the pressure within. That's always slightly stronger than any pressure without.

Owners say what they want and how they want it and of course the coaches will have to come in and put that in place. Yes, the pressure is there, and that's great. It makes the sport more professional and the jobs are better and give more security for players, coaches and everyone else.

If you've played the game and are now involved in the coaching side I think you really want to win because you're a competitive person. You want your teams to win, no coach wants his team to go out and not perform the way you've prepared them for. Owners that come into the game and expect instant success, whether it means money or we've got the best players, can't have it. It's all about chemistry and a working relationship. Yes there's pressure but it comes from within coaches themselves wanting their team to excel, and do well.

This season has been the most fun I've had since I won the shove ha'penny at the social club. The best in the club's history, it's not even close.

The last six years, at the end of every season, I've thought, is it worth it? It's been like hitting yourself with a hickory stick after a sauna, rolling in the snow - not my idea of pleasure. Then, after a couple of weeks I've missed it, and started thinking about the next season. It's what I've always done and I didn't want this season to end.

The uncertainty about being a coach's wife is actually one of the exciting things about it. Not knowing where you're going to be living in a year's time, never mind five.

I think before you commit to marriage you've got to realise you don't have a normal lifestyle. You've got to be very mobile and incredibly adaptable. For example, you've got to assess what the expectation level is in any given job. In a programme in the States, that might mean winning a championship, winning a place in the top four, wanting to be number one in the nation, these jobs all carry different levels with them.

Joe Whelton and Tom Becker are the best coaches I've played for. Both are very similar in the way they like their players to play.

Tom is a great believer in encouraging the ability of his players. He is not rigid about positions and likes his players to be able to do a bit of

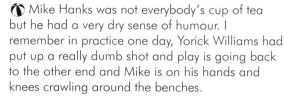

Bobby Knight is a good coach, no doubt about it. I think what makes him so good is the fact that he has instilled such traditional values in the team. Whether they have been there from the start, or whether he has adopted them from another coach, he has taken them all the way through with him.

At Indiana, for example, they wear the same warm-ups they have worn in all the time he has been there. Everything is based on tradition. I think the philosophy is, what goes around comes around when everything is based on tradition.

If a school has done well because of a certain system, it will continue to do well in the future, sooner or later. When you change that tradition, or when there isn't one established to start with, then your team is going to struggle. If you look at teams in this league, it's those with something of a tradition - however short it may be - that do well.

People who play for Coach Knight will tell you of the abuse, verbal and physical, you get playing for him, you know exactly what you are getting into when you go there. Because he is so traditional, the problems that players are going through there now are no different to what I, and hundreds of others, have gone through over the years.

It is just a question of saying, right I have four years of this and I can do it. Every young player that leaves the college because they think they cannot deal with Coach Knight soon realises there are worse people than him to play for. You might think he's not trying to help you, but what he is doing is trying to prepare you for life.

Firstly, I love the game. Secondly, I love teaching the game. I love the games but I love practice as much as the games. That, to me, is pure basketball. It's not a case of 'do we win? Do we lose?' It's really just getting the guys together, teaching the guys to play and compete. Then, to see a player grow, both as a player and a person, is a special thing for any coach at any level.

Mike Hanks was not everybody's cup of tea but he had a very dry sense of humour. I remember in practice one day, Yorick Williams had put up a really dumb shot and play is going back to the other end and Mike is on his hands and knees crawling around the benches.

Practice stopped and they asked Mike what was up. 'I think Yorick's lost his marbles,' said Mike. 'I'm just trying to help him find them!' The line was wasted on the players really, completely over their heads, they just kept looking at him in amazement.

I sit there during games, arguing calls, shouting and screaming and wondering what the hell I'm doing. I know I'm being stupid, I'm aware of everything I'm doing, I don't even know if I'm in the right or not, but I just can't help myself.

At least I'm conscious of that fact. I think there are some coaches who aren't. And I can always hope that one day I'll grow up.

O Trapping fingers in rims

The Wheelchair Game

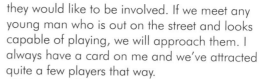

It's a close-knit community in wheelchair basketball, everybody knows each other but it's a very serious sport for a lot of people.

I was always a keen sportsman at school, playing football, cricket, rugby. I started playing basketball then but I have a rare form of congenital cancer and am now an amputee.

For most of us, wheelchair basketball is our only chance of sporting achievement. When I started, I didn't think I'd ever have any chance of representing my country in anything - now I've done it in basketball and fencing. It's a bonus for me to have done that.

The places I've been and the things I've seen over the years. We went to France for a tournament one year and stayed in a horrid hole of a place. It was like a POW camp.

One of the guys was made up because he found a commode chair which had little castors on it. So all the team took it in turns, pushing each other down the hill in it and falling out at the bottom. All I could think about was worrying that they weren't insured for it!

In the end, the able-bodied guy who was with us came off at the bottom and busted his ankle. He was the only one who got injured and all the guys were trying to convince him next day to get in a chair and play for us!

Normally I recruit players at the beginning of the season and again halfway through. I approach every club secretary and ask if they have any juniors - which is up to 22 in wheelchair basketball - and wherever we go I ask people if

they would like to be involved. If we meet any young man who is out on the street and looks capable of playing, we will approach them. I always have a card on me and we've attracted quite a few players that way.

Unfortunately, a lot of the bigger clubs don't want juniors hanging around. The snag is the older members on the team can tend to be very selfish and just want to concentrate on their own training. But obviously the juniors are the future of sport, any sport.

It's very difficult to get by in wheelchair basketball, and getting more so. We just about tick over from one game to the next. But the main thing is the cost of buying chairs.

They are specialist chairs and can cost anywhere from £1,100-£2,500. Most are custom-made specifically for the player, they have to be. You can get second-hand chairs, which a lot of players have to, but each chair should really be made to the user's requirements. They are very difficult to alter unless you have adjustable camber bars.

We have no sponsor at all, we depend on applying for grants and we are now a registered charity. But we would ideally like to spend the bits of money that comes in on equipment, rather than the running costs - paying refs, court hire - which are very high and which take up most of our income just now. We're more or less self-funding. Every Wednesday, everyone chips in to pay for court hire and, as most players are unable to work, that's quite difficult.

I coach the wheelchair game very much how I would the able-bodied version. In fact I plagiarise a lot of standard manuals. There is no big difference between the two, just the use of the chair that is different. An able-bodied player would be able to come and sit in a chair and make his shot.

From the grassroots level, we do taster days, beginner courses, getting kiddies from schools,

64

around, you found the game gradually building up and in 1963 we started the Yorkshire women's league.

We started with about six teams, mostly university, and got it going with that. Doncaster was another of the earlier teams, there has always been a good basketball tradition there. Word of mouth spread through the men's leagues and by '76 we had started the National League, this is our 21st anniversary.

I played until I got to a stage, at about the age of 34, when my husband told me I had to make my mind up between playing and coaching because I wasn't doing either properly. It was very difficult to get a coach to stay with you more than a couple of years so I decided to concentrate solely on coaching.

Since we started, the Hatters have won eight National Cups, seven National Leagues and four Championship titles. We've done the triple twice, we're going for a third successive one this year, so from very humble beginnings we've not done too badly. The '90s have probably been our years but for many years we struggled. You honestly wouldn't believe what we have travelled to matches in over the years.

If we were lucky, we would get a minibus, but we weren't always that lucky. It depended on whether one of our players, who worked for the students' union, could get their bus or not. If not, we had to hire or get hold of things you wouldn't be allowed to use now. We used to hire a van, stick cushions and sleeping bags in it and pile in the back.

The times we've had to get changed in the back of the bus because we were lost, didn't have directions, and were late. That seemed to happen particularly when we were playing in London. We'd create quite a stir, ten women getting undressed in the back of a minibus, the fellas' eyes would be popping out..

And the stuff we used to wear. We played in a sort of polyester dress, we didn't wear shorts in

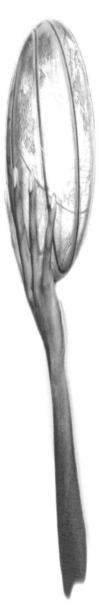

those days. I show the girls what we used to wear some time - I'm bringing a dress out for the end of season do - and they can't believe it.

Once we had just changed the clocks and we were playing at Southampton the next day. Of course, one of the younger girls forgot to change hers and missed us at the meeting point. Somehow she convinced her mum and dad to drive her all the way down to Southampton, even though she didn't know where the gym was. She never did find us.

I remember vividly playing a Yorkshire League match at Hull one year and travelling in a mobile vegetable shop that one of us owned. I spent all the trip sitting on a sack of potatoes, absolutely frozen stiff in the depths of winter. We were all laughing at each other and I said, 'I ache so much, I've been sitting on a sack of spuds all the way.' One of the girls turned round and said, 'You're lucky, you've had potatoes, I've been sitting on a sack of carrots!'

O Going to get lynched

The Officials

🏀 A good referee is somebody that has played a reasonable standard and got a feel for the game, understands what players and coaches are trying to do and is consistent in his, or her, calls.

A lot of it at our level is man-management. It's one of the most important, and most difficult, aspects of the job. You can have someone who has read the rule book inside out and can quote it back to front, but if he doesn't have a feel for people and for the game you can put him out on the floor and he would be crap.

You can't teach that, of course, you've really got to learn by your own mistakes. You can't wrap a young ref in cotton wool. You have to put him among the big boys and get him to screw up a few times, to learn from his mistakes.

🏀 I think there's a general agreement that standards in refereeing need improving. There seems to be a lack of will and lack of resources to provide people with the opportunity to improve, that's what I feel. We have to do something financially to help them improve, otherwise it will continue to be a problem.

There is a small fund put to one side, £15,000 I believe, to help in the development of referees in this country but that is a very small amount of money when you consider that referees at division three football matches earn £185 a game.

We need fast tracking for our referees. Identify the people with the right psychological make-up and ability and fast track them so they can be up to the right standard in a couple of years time, rather than ten years time.

We need a proper structure for our referees, an element of accountability, and a system that will reward the better refs financially.

🏀 I made grade one in '87, I was 27 then. I started late and people like me and Richard Stokes and Keith Williams invested heavily in our refereeing careers, in terms of sacrifice and expense. It's better now, but there just wasn't the support back then. Holidays, time off, money, you have to sacrifice all that sort of stuff because at the end of the day, it's how much you want it. And I want it bad.

I went to FIBA in '95. I was supposed to go to a camp in Slovenia in the May but the EBBA lost my form or something and it was September before I got out to a camp in Brussels.

There were 23 other candidates from around the world and just 12 were chosen. They just happened to all come from countries who didn't have refs on the list already, so it was obviously a political decision that had been taken before we even got there.

I still regard myself as one of the best in this country, I see some of the guys with blue badges and think they are out of shape and don't work as hard as I do at the game. It's not so much political at our level because we all tend to stick together, but when you get to the FIBA level it's very political.

You just have to look at the appointments for Olympic Games, Olympic Finals, that sort of thing. Guys from Czechoslovakia, the old Yugoslavia, Greece. It's all politics.

But I'd love to be a part of it. I know, just from when I've been abroad with various England teams and refereed along with other guys, I've watched them and wondered how they've ever achieved the badge.

🏀 You hear stories all the time about attempted bribery in Europe but I don't think it's anywhere near as prevalent as it was in the '70s and '80s.

And there is no doubt about it, wherever you go in Europe, teams breath a sigh of relief when they know an English guy is refereeing.

In the old days, if you were the visiting team in Europe you knew you had no chance whatsoever of winning unless you were a really exceptional team. Now the playing field is a lot more even and teams know that they are going to get a straight game out of the English guy. The same may not apply to the other ref, but it does to the Brit.

🏀 Being a table official isn't always easy. Certainly not a few weeks ago when this bunch of clowns from Sheffield were screaming at us at Chester.

There was an incident with the 30 second clock, whether or not it should have been reset, and I thought we were going to get lynched by the Sheffield crowd. I told someone from Sheffield to disappear in rather choice language. This is my last season of table officiating, I won't miss it.

🏀 The table looks complicated in big games but it isn't. There is a three-person crew - a scorekeeper who basically records all the information in the scorebook, the timekeeper who times the game and the 30 second operator who operates the shot clock.

The scorekeeper is also responsible for time-outs and the correct procedure for substitutions, knowing when teams can and cannot sub during games.

I'm still amazed that some players don't know the rules about time-outs, substitutions. Even some coaches don't, actually even some refs, as well. You often get abuse from coaches wanting to call a time-out when they're not entitled to.

🏀 Statistics are becoming increasingly important in the modern game. A coach can break down the statistical information from the game, or even from training sessions, and see whether a particular player is playing the correct offensive position, whether people are rebounding in certain positions.

It's a game of possession, when you have it the other team can't score, and stats are becoming increasingly important in analysing the game.

Take football. It's becoming more important there. You see on the television, Liverpool are said to have had 58 per cent of the possession, so many shots on target. In basketball, that information has to be even more detailed. A starter who scores two points in 20 minutes may obviously not be contributing as much as a guy who comes off the bench and scores 15 points in the first five minutes.

You have to be strictly neutral in these things, such as handing out assists, which is easy when you've seen as many games as I have. I used to get hauled to one side by players complaining about their stats, but you stand your ground - and ask them how many turnovers they committed.

🏀 London Towers were playing at Chester this season and my assistant Robbie Peers had been watching their big American Joe Hooks on tape and told me that every time he caught the ball he travelled with it.

'We're going to have to point this out to the refs,' he said. The problem was that we couldn't just pick up a phone and complain about it, so we hatched this plan.

Alan Richardson was one of the refs and he'd asked us to book him a hotel to stay after the game. So I called Alan and he came to the phone and asked who it was.

'It's Burt,' I said. 'I've got your hotel details for the weekend. Have you got a pen ready?'

Alan said he had, so I read out very slowly: 'This ... is ... Burt ... from ... Joe ... Hooks ... travels ... every ... time ... he ... touches .... the ... ball!'

The pair of us cracked up but Robbie and I thought we had made a point. The post script to

71

all this, of course, was that Hooks didn't even play against us! He was injured.

☎ Pete Mintoft was coaching England against Ireland, in a cadet men's international in Cork a few years ago. I was refereeing and England were winning by one with a few seconds left and Pete called a time-out on a dead ball.

The Irish ref was Sean Tracey who was standing with the ball next to the Irish huddle while I was stood at the table. The next thing I hear is the 'thud thud thud' of a bouncing ball and I look up to see the Irish team running down court with the English still in their huddle.

I said to Mintoft, 'You'd better get your lads out there pretty quick, the Irish ref has put the ball in before time.' So they rush on, there's about four seconds left by this stage, the Irish put the shot up on the hooter, the ball hits the ring, bounces up and an Irish kid jumps up and tips the ball in the basket.

I'm the trail ref so Tracey comes up court and signals two points. Well, Mintoft understandably went berserk. He was standing next to a chair, he kicked it and, I'm not joking, this chair went like an exocet, straight up in the air and clattered to the floor about ten feet away.

Pete was screaming, saying that there was no way it could be a basket. I said, 'Pete, don't worry, the basket wasn't good. I'll sort it out.'

By this stage, Sean is at the table signalling two points, so I go over and tell him that the game was over and there was no way those two points could stand.

'No, no, no,' said Sean. 'It's two points.'

'Sean,' I said. 'FIBA rules clearly state that is no basket.'

'Yes,' said Sean. 'You're right. FIBA rules state that. But this is Cork and Cork rules say TWO POINTS!'

And that was that ... England and Pete lost by one point.

☎ I was refereeing a game with Billy earlier this season and, as usual, he was riding me a little bit and arguing every call that came along. That's fine, that's Bill and that's what our relationship is like.

But after a while I'd had enough, so I said, 'Billy, you're really going to have to put a sock in it.' But, of course, five minutes later he's at it again and really getting on my nerves.

'Billy,' I said. 'That's it, I'm not going to listen to you any more.'

'Typical,' said Billy. 'You never listen to me.'

So that was it. I gave him a 'T' and, quick as a flash, Billy came straight back at me. 'What was that for?' he asked looking all hurt. 'You said you weren't listening to me.'

☎ Will Jones is one of the best - or worst, depending how you look at it - practical jokers in the business. One year he was refereeing the Roy Curtis Tournament in Dublin with George Valentine, a Scottish guy, and as is often the case, everyone went out on the night time and got hammered.

Will switched the nominations to make sure that George got the early game, starting at 10am, and then told him it had been done by the organisers. Reluctantly, George crawled out of bed thinking he could just about get through the match in one piece. Of course, the inevitable happened, and the game is in the Guinness Book of Records as the longest basketball match of all-time - it went to five over-time periods or something!

The next day, Will and George were refereeing a semi-final between a Russian team and an American touring team which, as normal, was like World War Three. A guy goes driving down the lane, gets fouled and throws the ball up, with George unsighted.

George turns to Will and looks as if to ask if the basket was good, so Will nods and mouths, 'Yeh, the ball went in.' So George goes over to the table

with his arm flying like a fast bowler, indicating 'basket good.'

Of course, the place goes mad because the ball had not gone in at all. George had to shout across - never a good thing to do - 'Will, did it go in?'

'Of course it bloody didn't,' said Will.

That's Will for you.

🏀 The abuse you take from people is part and parcel of the game. In some arenas now, because of the noise and the entertainment package they provide, you don't hear half the rubbish anyway.

I look at it from two perspectives. One, if I wasn't good enough to be doing these games I wouldn't have done as many as I have, year after year. And two, if someone wants to pay £5-6 to watch a game and hurl abuse at me, then at least I am keeping them entertained!

At the end of the day, Joe Public doesn't know what you're doing, what you're trying to achieve because they've not been on the court, got the qualification. And they are supporting the team, you're the official and of course it's your fault if the team loses.

At the start of the season we thought we would have to communicate more with players and coaches and I don't have a problem with that. But when coaches want to stop the game and argue every call, then the pendulum has swung the other way too far. It needs to swing more back towards the officials, or at least to the centre.

The worst coach at the moment, for his sheer moaning, is Billy. Surprise, surprise. Three of the most constructive, who will give you very positive feedback in the comments they write on the report and tell you when you've had a bad one or a good one, are Nurse, Brandon and Burton. Very fair, honest people.

I do feel sorry for the teams down at the bottom of the league. Coach Lewis, Hibbs, Vince. So I probably stretch the elastic a bit more with them because I know they are going through the motions and just want to win so bad. As long as I talk to them during the game and tell them what I'm doing, there is no problem.

🏀 Colin Gerrard and myself were refereeing a game in Doncaster some time ago and I went down to pick CG up in Teesside on my way down. As usual, we were in a rush, so as he was leaving he just grabbed a pile of kit and threw it all in his kit bag.

It wasn't until we got to the game that he realised he had picked up the wrong pair of trousers. Instead of his usual game trousers, he had a pair that hadn't been tailored, they were miles too long for him.

Anyway, Fred Matthews came in at this point and told CG, 'Don't worry, I'll sort them out for you.' So he disappeared brandishing a pair of scissors as he went.

A few minutes later, Colin was walking on to court, alongside me, wearing the worst pair of trousers you have seen in your life. They barely covered his shins, Fred had made such a bad job of cutting them to size.

🏀 I remember during the early nineties when there was talk of a possible referees' strike. Myself and various other league office staff, with no refereeing qualifications, spent weeks driving around with grey referee kit in the boot of our cars just in case. Thankfully it never came down to it, but the mind boggles what it would have been like if we'd been called into action. Frightening.

🏀 I used to play National League in Wirral and Liverpool and I played for England schoolgirls until I got a back injury which prevented me from playing at a good standard. That was six years ago and I wanted to remain involved in the game.

I was a local league ref and decided I wanted to do the National League and now I'm one of three

No Bud League

qualified women in the country and I'm off to a refs' camp in the States soon which will hopefully help me even more.

I do everything apart from the Bud League where I'm not qualified yet, that all depends on whether I'm selected. I'd like to think I will be. I'm hoping to be the next female Bud League official. There isn't one at the minute, there was Chris Knowles but she retired.

On the whole I am treated very positively on the circuit, people are really positive towards me. The odd one will not have any respect for me but there is nothing you can do about that and the rest are really good.

I don't want to be treated any differently, but then again I've got to realise I'm a woman out there. One of the best pieces of advice I had was from Nick Stonard who said use what you've got to get where you want. If that means a smile on court to get you out of a sticky situation, then I do it.

I don't find myself in too many of those sticky situations as I get more experienced but I did when I first started. I think I was a bit paranoid about things people said to me. Things that weren't meant to be funny I would take the wrong way.

For example, I would find it offensive if a player tapped me on the bum after a call but a player would do that to a ref if he was a bloke. Now, I interpret that sort of thing as a player treating me just the same as a male ref and that's the way I want it.

I love refereeing because you're out there, you're involved in the game. Everyone says to me it is a power trip because I'm a girl out there in charge of all these guys but it's not that.

When you're out there you're involved in the game, you're not there to control it, you're there to help it get along and I love the banter, the real buzz you get when you make a right call, know you have, and the guy you've called it on winks at you to let you know you called it right.

I was in Ireland with the Chester Jets at a

tournament the Christmas before last and there was an incident I've become quite famous for. Ricardo Leonard was playing for an Irish team, against a Russian team, and the gym was absolutely packed. Fans were on the baseline, sideline, you had to ref on court.

I made this call on Ricardo and he just stood there and stared at me. I'm a big girl, but Ricardo's massive and he just snarled at me, 'You know what girl, you must be a good ***, because you sure can't ref.'

Quick as a flash I hit back, 'One thing's for sure, Ricardo, you'll never find out, will you?'

I've become quite famous for that, but the point is a player will respect that more, if you can make a comment to diffuse a situation rather than hitting someone with a 'T'. Of course, I'm also coming at this from a different perspective and can get away with some things male refs couldn't.

That's why I'm going over to the States, more than anything to focus on the philosophy and man-management of refereeing.

I like all the things I get out of it, travelling up and down the country all the time, meeting a lot of good friends, having a good time. Referees are an especially small group and we all know each other.

If I had the choice now between playing for England and refereeing a Budweiser game, I'd go for the refereeing all the time. I played local league last season but it is refereeing for me now.

In ten years time I'd like to be a FIBA ref, doing men's games, which is something we are not allowed to do at the moment. Chris Knowles is the only Englishwoman who's been on the FIBA list so far and that is why she quit. She found there was such a lot of resistance, from the old school. But I think the game is generally more supportive of women these days.

○ I was a panda at the National Cup Final

The Entertainers

◐ I was conned into becoming a mascot, really. I work for the sound company that does the PA at Shark games and they asked me if I wanted to earn some extra cash while I was hanging around doing nothing.

I start Mexican waves, squirt people with water pistols, some intentional, others not, and it's amazing the response you get from kids. Many of them come up asking for your autograph.

I'm blind while I'm doing everything, which is a distinct disadvantage, and it's hard for me to get my arms up. I'm trying to shrink the head, but they don't seem to like the idea. I was a panda at the National Cup Final which I thought was horrible so there are worse things in life than being a shark.

◐ I'm a trampolinist and used to go to gym club which is where the club made contact, asking if anybody could do a back-flip and somersault and who was a little bit crazy. I fitted the description so that was it.

I like basketball and this is a fun way to get involved and meet lots of nice, different people. I like communicating with people and I get a lot of enjoyment out of doing what I do.

The thing people always ask is if it's hot inside the costume, and yes, it is. But the worst thing is the hammerhead that I have to wear, when I'm doing somersaults on the floor I can't see where I'm landing so it's a little bit scary as well.

Once I fell straight on my head, but I quickly made out that was part of the act and everybody though it was normal, they didn't realise I was really flopping on the floor.

When me and Sharky were dancing and boxing once to the Rocky music, my fist went straight through the mouth of his costume and gave him a nose bleed. Sharky wasn't too pleased as you can imagine.

The best thing that happened to me as Hammerhead was when some lady had a new-born baby at the game and asked if she could have his picture taken with me. That was brilliant.

◐ I'm still deciding what to call what I do. 'Juggler' is too specific, 'Ball Handler' is not broad enough. I've not thought of a title as yet. I don't know, 'Basketball entertainer,' 'Basketball showman,' might be nearer the mark.

There is a woman in America, Tanya Criever, I try to base myself on what she's doing but not many people here know about her and I've only got about 15 seconds of her act on video tape.

She has been a big inspiration, but how I got into it was through playing basketball. I started at 14 and for the next four years I really concentrated on wanting to dunk the ball, you know, the showman side of things.

That preoccupied me and took over my ambitions in the game. I started to notice guys blowing by me in games and realised all of a sudden that I was rubbish! So I went into doing the dumb tricks, you know spinning the ball on my finger.

Where I went to school in Somerset this was something of a novelty, I guess, so I started getting more attention for doing these sort of dumb things than I ever did from playing. I started loving the attention, moved onto tricks with two balls, bouncing them between my legs.

◐ Yuri asked me down to the Sharks last season, he knew I did some radio stuff and coached a school team and wanted someone to do the announcing. Coming from West Yorkshire, I knew about the Sharks and with the EBBA being based

in Leeds, it's hard not to take to the game in this part of the world just now.

The thing I like most about Sheffield is that they put on a great show and it would be nice to see more clubs moving into these sort of arenas and doing similar things. I know there is talk of a Budweiser League team starting in Leeds and that would create a real buzz in the county.

When I'm announcing, I try not to commentate, it's not the type of sport that lends itself to that style with basketball being so free-flowing. You would just be describing a basket and who did what and by the time you had finished, play would be at the other end and you would have missed another basket.

I also try to get both sides into the commentary. You know, 'Who's here tonight from Newcastle?' 'Who's supporting Sheffield tonight?' Basically, you try to have fun and involve everyone even if we are that little bit partisan towards Sheffield.

The only thing I can compare it to in sports is the Rugby League Cup Final at Wembley when you have sets of supporters from both clubs mixing freely with no sense of trouble, just having a giggle.

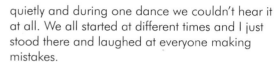 The first game we did, at Pond's Forge, was awful. In those days, we just danced, we didn't put any personality or thought into it. The first game, one of us got the dance completely wrong and just stood there motionless. At one stage, I was just doing my own thing, different to everyone else.

Last year, one of the girls ran off halfway through a routine. We thought she'd injured her leg but it was just because she had got the dance wrong.

One of the other cheerleaders slipped on one of the player's wet towels and dislocated her jaw! She just pushed it back in and carried on for the whole match! After she had finished dancing she just broke down and cried with the pain. She was 14.

It's not so easy when Sky are here televising the games because the music has to be played more

quietly and during one dance we couldn't hear it at all. We all started at different times and I just stood there and laughed at everyone making mistakes.

Sam's the leader and she started at the beginning of the routine while others started in the middle. It was the first Sky game, we were really trying to get people in and impress them and it was a complete fiasco. We don't do that particular dance any more.

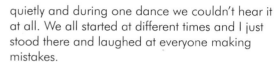 I think cheerleaders and the whole entertainment package are now integral to basketball at the professional level. At the end of the day, most sport appeals to males, so often you need other things to entice women, young girls, along, so that they can feel part of it as well.

We now have a series of clinics, called the Rising Stars, to give girls a taste of cheerleading and the first two we held had over 300 people turn up. That's the way forward. If you're taking basketball into school and teaching kids the game, there are going to be children - girls in particular - who just aren't interested. But if a nine-year-old girl has the chance to get dressed up, have her hair and make-up done, she's in her element. So, get them interested in the entertainment side of basketball, get the whole family involved.

We're also looking to change that impression that boys play the game while girls jump up and down on the sidelines. I've brought in a gymnastics coach and want to use boys doing stunt work as part of the act, as they do in American colleges.

We've been into schools and, at one in Cheadle Hulme, the girls now go out in their t-shirts and pom-poms and cheer for their own school football team. Hopefully when we start having weekly cheerleader camps we will see lots more young cheerleaders out there.

born in the usa

"overpaid, overfed, oversexed, and over here**"**

tommy trinder

It's a hell of a long way from Fog Lane to the NBA

The American Dream

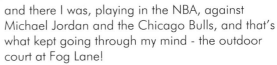

Everyone dreams of making it in the NBA when they're a kid in the States. If you find an American ball player who tells you he didn't, then he's lying.

No-one wants to think they are not going to make it. It's like the fire that drives you to keep playing, even now. I bet there are a lot of guys playing in England right now who still think and dream about making it.

I think that's why you still put in the hard work after all these years, the hope of getting better and maybe getting noticed. That's what I learned at any early age - that hard work doesn't guarantee you anything, but without it you don't have a chance.

Right now, I just want to do the best I can in the European leagues and better myself as a player and a person and then look to the future, make future plans and set future goals for myself.

I just try to learn from the experience I'm having, from the travelling and the living away from home. I love that aspect of it and I've always said, you've got to be happy doing what you're doing.

When I was a kid growing up in Manchester I used to play at Fog Lane, the only outdoor court for miles around, even though it meant a long bus ride to get there.

I used to beat up on all the other kids quite easily, purely because I was so much bigger and stronger than they were and I used to tell them: 'One day I'll be playing against Michael Jordan in the NBA.'

They laughed in my face and pointed out it's a hell of a long way from Fog Lane to the NBA.

But you know what, it wasn't too many years later and there I was, playing in the NBA, against Michael Jordan and the Chicago Bulls, and that's what kept going through my mind - the outdoor court at Fog Lane!

It was weird to be out there at the start of the game. It was almost like an out-of-body experience, hearing the announcer say 'Starting at centre ... John Amaechi!!'

I remember thinking, I have seen this on TV, now it's happening to me. That was the culmination of years and years of hard work and dreams - a dream that I had no right to achieve, given the route I had taken.

I appreciate it now more looking back because at the time playing in the NBA was such a shock to the system. I was ready at the start of the year, I had lost 20 pounds, gained two and a half inches vertical leap. But by mid-season I was really tired.

I was lucky to have some good veterans around me like Michael Cage, who became a close personal friend. And my experience has not put me off the NBA. I moved to Greece for financial reasons and because I don't like being mediocre at anything I do. Last season, I was an average NBA player. Now I am a much better all-round player.

Andy Betts came back for a week on his spring break from college and I've spoken to NBA scouts regarding him. The kid has a lot of potential. But I remember Chuck Daly telling me, potential gets coaches the sack! What the heck does potential do?

But his potential means he has a bright future, whether at that level or not, who knows? If he does put in the work, I could see a really bright future and NBA scouts would be interested. I was one myself and know exactly what they're looking for and anytime you've got someone who is 7'1" who can move, they are interested.

He's also aggressive, he isn't bashful, which is another plus. He's a raw player, he hasn't been

taught a lot, he's only been in the game three years. That's the downside, but that's the upside as well because he could really just take off.

It's going to be up to him. If he spends 24/7 doing the things it takes I could see him playing big-time basketball. But I've seen millions of kids reach that stage and not put in the time or have the right people around to force them into that situation.

He's at Long Beach State so we will know more in a year, you've got to give it some time. But at this time next year we can assess whether he's made a good move going there. He's only 19, he'll only be 20 in a year, so if it doesn't work out over there, heck I'd take him. He's a Leicester boy, his family come to games and we've enjoyed having him in the club. He's a great kid.

🏀 I think what happened to me in the NBA was a case of a bit too much too soon. I definitely wasn't ready for it and the team made a poor start to the season with me starting for them, which didn't help.

It was a bad situation for me because it was difficult enough as it was to start games in the NBA without the fact that the team as a whole wasn't playing well. It was all a major adjustment, a major change to anything I had been used to.

I expected everything to be a lot easier than it turned out to be. I had prepared myself pre-season in Phoenix and came in playing very well and felt ready. But, as a consequence of that, I was also extremely tired and by the time we got 20 games into the season it had started to wear on me.

In no way does college ball prepare you. You think you are ready but when it comes down to it, you just aren't. There are so many more games, the standard of competition is so much higher. In college, you can relax for the first nine games of the season because the schedule is usually weighted so you play some terrible teams at the start. In the pros, it's not like that, especially for a

rookie. You have to play your hardest from the start.

You have maybe one day off in nine or ten, the rest of the time you are either practising or travelling. Now I can look back and say it was all a positive experience but there were times during the season when I wasn't really sure that would be the case.

I had doubts in my own ability, I didn't know whether I really wanted to do this for an extended period of time. There were days I didn't know whether I was even good enough to do it for an extended period of time.

And life in the NBA is not really as glamorous as people think it is. Everything about it is not as good as you would imagine. Every basketball player in every country wishes he could play in the NBA but when it comes down to it, unless you are at the very top level of elite guys it does very much become a job. That's not all bad, of course. You've got to make a living and there are a lot worse ways of doing that.

There is not one thing I could point to, it is just the whole package of life in the NBA. It just is not as attractive as it would seem.

Having said that, I wouldn't swap my experiences for anything. It took me a long time to get there and it is still my goal to get back there in the very near future.

🏀 I was offered the head coach job at Derby so I went off there because I knew I wanted to coach. I think we finished 12-12 that season, which was the best record they had ever had. They had come up to the League four years before and were winning three or four games a year. But we beat Manchester twice, which they'd never done before, and beat everybody that year apart from Kingston when Ernest Lee missed a 15 footer at the buzzer and we lost by one.

My starting line-up that year was me, Ernest, Terry Manghum, Tim Lascelles, Dave Roper, with Martin

Ford off the bench and Andy Tucker seventh man. I don't know how we won a game that season, but we played our backsides off ... and Ernest was awesome.

What an unbelievable scorer he was, just a scoring machine. 6'4", 225 pounds, but he had real tunnel vision, once he started going to the basket he couldn't see or do anything else but get the shot off.

The sad thing about Ernest is he killed himself, jumped off the Sacramento Bridge . Why? NBA dreams I think. I mean I don't know that for a fact but he had played in the same high school league as Kevin Johnson, who's now a great NBA player, and Ernest was MVP of that league.

We all shared a house and I went in his room one time and written on his wall was, 'KJ, 11.5 over 4. Damn!' It was a reference to a new contract Johnson had signed with Phoenix that paid him $11.5 MILLION over four years, and there was Ernest on a 160 quid a week in England.

He got drafted, or was with the Kings or Clippers in the NBA, I can't remember which. He made a lot of cuts but wasn't really that close to making it in the League. He didn't defend or pass the ball that well, but boy could he score. He led NCAA Division Two in scoring for three years in a row.

After my year, he went back to the States and he never played and I never heard from him again. I tried to call him a few times, but could never get through. The next thing, I get like an eight page fax sent to me at the college where I was coaching from the Sacramento Chronicle, or whatever, telling his story.

○ Brands on my leg, my arm, my chest

College Ball

○

🏀 I'd compare the pro game here to college ball in the States. There are a lot of good players which means you've got to come out ready to play every night. That's one reason I prefer it here to Ireland. The other is that there are more games. Here, it's three or four practices a week and one or two games. There, it was a couple of practices and one game. You can't improve your basketball if you're not playing and practising all the time.

🏀 In the States, you play high school, you play college, then you retire or play professionally. That is one of the reasons why there is such an emphasis on college basketball in the States.

For instance, when we travelled to road games at UConn there would be a minimum of ten journalists following our team around because there was no professional sports team there. We played regularly in front of 15,000 home crowds and just about every game was televised live and every single game was on the radio.

The pressure from that can work either way. My college career was the biggest thrill of my life, but it also wasn't a normal college existence, I missed out on a lot of fun - which I made up for later - but it really was a lot of pressure for a young man to handle.

In the beginning it's the greatest thing in the world but, as your college career goes on, you have studies to contend with and you have a life after basketball to think about and it becomes increasingly hard to cope.

Sometimes, I remember really being afraid because we had a game that night. It wasn't the big games that were the problems, more the little

games against the University of Maine or New Hampshire when the fear of failure was the motivation rather than the fun of competition. There was a lot of pressure, a lot of scrutiny in the media.

🏀 I went to a college that was not suited to me. I went to a school in Nashville, Tennessee. In hindsight, Vanderbilt was a good school but after one semester, I was averaging two points, two rebounds a game and had a 2.2 grade point average. A year later, after transferring to Penn State, I had a 3.5 GPA and was an Academic All-American.

For me, the coach was the big sticking point, it was as simple as that. We never communicated, never had any understanding. I thought I was going to be a great basketball player but he started our relationship by telling me he thought I should have gone to a Division Three college. That was a problem, right there.

I have dozens of high schools and colleges I could send English kids to. I've just helped one guy, from my old club Stockport Atlas, spend a year at high school in Toledo. He is never going to play in the NBA, he won't play at a Division One college, but he has had a great experience in his life, of going to school in a foreign country and playing a lot of basketball in the best possible circumstances.

🏀 Canada was more laid back, sort of a middle ground between here and the States. It wasn't crazy, like New York, but a quicker pace of life than England. I liked the mixture. The best aspects of the US, the best aspects of here, and not as crazy as the States. The balance is pretty good.

In terms of coaching, prep school wasn't that great - better than I could have hoped for here but, having spoken to guys who've been to the States, it wasn't as intense as the US system. University in Halifax, Nova Scotia, was pretty much the same. Remember, ice hockey is the main sport over there.

It was a pretty good way to combine schooling and playing ball, playing guys who are good athletes. The game is a lot more established over there, better organised, the competition is intense, serious. Basketball is part of the mainstream, sporting culture.

I benefited as a player, practising every day, playing guys who have grown up playing all their lives, there was no way but to improve. The place I went, the level of coaching was pretty good and the coach a good teacher. That's what swung me in the school's direction, rather than going to the States where it is more a case of polishing what skills you start with. I had played too little basketball for that.

🏀 I received my 'brands' when I was at college at Wayne State. I was a member of Omega Psi Phi, an all-black male fraternity and branding is optional but I did it to let everybody know how important it is to me.

We live by four cardinal principles - manhood, scholarship, perseverance and uplift - and once you are in, it's a lifetime thing. I did it to let everybody know how much I appreciated belonging and I try to apply the principles to my everyday life.

We are all over the world. Michael Jordan is in the fraternity, Jessie Jackson, John Salley, Shaquille O'Neal and we have different chapters all around the world, not just sports, in many different fields.

To actually do the brand, everybody shapes their own irons to whatever size they want. It's a third degree burn and only takes a second to do. It doesn't actually hurt that much because it is so hot it kills the nerves in the area. The only time you feel it is in the healing process when you have to make sure it stays clean so the wound doesn't become infected. I've had a tattoo as well and that hurt a lot more. I'd take a brand over a tattoo any day.

I've got brands on my leg, my arm, my chest. I've worked pretty damn hard to get where I am so these really say that I'm proud to belong to my frat.

A fraternity is an elite group of guys, all standing for what's good. We're all about business, but we do have our fun. We do community service, raise money to do different things. When you're in college you can't do much but we would go to hospitals and offer our services there, or help the old or homeless at holiday times.

Once you leave, there is another group to take your place, but when you move on into the world you still try to help. I spent a lot of time working in community services with kids and that's why I still love them so much and try and do what I can to help them.

I was fortunate. When I was growing up in Kalamazoo, Michigan, it was either drugs or sports, there was no in between. I had an older brother who was a keen basketball player and I followed him everywhere. I could have picked drugs but luckily I did everything he did and played ball.

I've seen my friends die, I've seen them do drugs, seen them sell drugs. I've been shot at, I've almost been car-jacked when I've been back home. I have been at the park, when I was a kid, and seen a guy I was with shot in the ankle in a drive-by. These are kids doing all this and that's why I feel so strongly about trying to teach and help as many kids as I come into contact with.

❶ It might sound harsh, but if it wasn't for basketball, I'd be dead, in jail, or doing some kind of business I shouldn't. I've been caught up in the middle of gunfights, chased by the cops and locked up. I couldn't tell you what the friends I had back then are doing now. Some may have passed away if they didn't find a means of escape like me. My older brother was killed two years ago this December. He was just in the wrong place at the wrong time and was shot three times.

That's what made my mind up, I knew I had to get out. Life in the Bronx can swallow you up. Luckily I was at a high school where I could play ball. I played with a group of guys each day for longer and longer periods and began to improve. I realised that I could get to college on a scholarship, it was a means to get out safely.

You have to understand that it's very hard for a young black male to get a good education and a job there. I was lucky, others - like my brother - weren't.

○ Reaching the big time

Coming to England

● This is probably more funny to an American than a British guy, but I will always remember my debut for Derby, down at London Docklands, which was a real tough old venue in those days.

I had just been in the country for five days, this was my first game in England, I didn't know where the hell I was or what I was doing and the fat guy who does the announcing down there was doing the P.A. The place was packed, hundreds of school kids were in, and just before he starts to announce the teams, the P.A. breaks down.

So the guy just walks onto court and starts yelling the names out. I remember turning to Ernest Lee and saying, 'Boy, I've really reached the big time here. What the hell have I got myself into?'

● Before I came here I knew nothing about English basketball. I knew they had it but I couldn't have named you two teams. I think generally, Americans are ignorant of European basketball, English in particular, but then they have the best in the world, the NBA.

The NBA market their teams in this country so the people know who the Chicago Bulls are. The London Towers are not marketed in the States, and I doubt they ever will be, so no-one knows who they are. And, of course, apart from the NBA they have college ball which attracts huge interest.

● I compare basketball here to soccer in the States. Both are in the growing stages and both are getting more and more popular, especially with the kids who play it in their millions.

The World Cup in the States was a big help to football, it was able to grow quite a bit over there

because of it and I hope the NBA will have the same effect helping basketball to grow over here. That is where the four American rule is helping basketball in Britain, in terms of young fans seeing a better product, better players.

● The thing with the British fan is that he or she doesn't really know the game that well yet. They don't know the calls, what's going on. They just look for the ball going into the basket and who has got the most points at the end of the night wins - that's how much some fans understand.

The more they come to understand it, the more they will look for the moves, the offences that are being run, they will look for the things that make good teams - the picks and screens, the offensive patterns, the defensive intensity.

The thing with basketball is that a lot of people just follow the ball, when they should look at what goes on off the ball.

● The reason I got involved in the Basketball Players' Association was that I enjoy living in England and, regardless of whether I'm playing basketball or not, I'd like to stay here.

If you're in a place or a situation like that and feel you can make a difference, a chance, to people around you, you should. When I started talking to players around the league, part of my doctorate degree I'm studying for here in Manchester, I found many players were complaining about things.

England has been good to me, the people have been good to me, and I don't think it matters whether it's an English person or an American person running the union as long as the union looks out for the British player, and that's what I definitely try to do. I hope I'm looking out for all players.

A lot of black leaders I've studied - Malcolm X, Martin Luther King, Louis Farrakhan - people who preach you have to give back to your community.

then they have to go back somewhere to be developed. There is no shortage of kids, but a shortage of coaches, the right people to take them to that next level. When we were coming through we had Mike Burton and Joe Forber to get us to the next level. There are not enough of those types of people now.

As far as spectators go, and as far as parity goes, having four work permits has been a good idea. But for the overall good of English basketball, I think there are going to have to be changes. Looking at the national team, players are playing for their country who don't even get 15 minutes for their club team because they are in competition with five foreigners. I can't see English players benefiting at all from the rule. I don't understand why we don't go back to FIBA's rules. I'm not a lawyer but I've got a pretty damn good idea that it might be illegal not to follow their rules!

I think there should be two work permits per team and then, under the Bosman rules, teams can fill up their bench with Brits or other EU players. A decent European is just as good as a lot of Americans would be and it would be better for the English players.

You see, if we were going by the old rules, local guys like Yorick Williams and Mike Bernard would be playing a lot more for us. As it is, there is an obvious pressure to play your Americans. People ask why Mike and Yorick haven't played as much this season as last. Well that's the reason.

TV is so important in this. Sky likes the idea of four or five foreigners running around out there but, having been a national coach in two countries, I can say that without a doubt, English players will suffer down the line.

The thing you cannot forget is that this is a business for the players, it's their job, their living and their family's living.

People have said that the four Americans rule means guys are just going to come here and try and put up big numbers so they can get a better move and more money somewhere else in Europe. That's quite possible, it's also quite natural.

It's very easy, from a marketing point of view, to say that the Americans have been fantastic, great. The argument, of course, is that they are costing English players jobs. But those players who have had to go and play in the National League - the likes of Dave Roper, Steve Darlow - well, with the best will in the world, they are not players people are going to pay money to watch. That may be harsh, but I wouldn't pay a fiver just to watch those players and the fact is Sky TV wouldn't stay interested for long if that was the case.

I would have loved to have stuck around but, with the five Americans rule, the stakes had been raised. We sat down and had a chat at the end of the season and Jim said he would have loved to have kept me but he couldn't give me an answer until late in the summer and by that time I had other irons in the fire in terms of work.

I took them which is just as well because I don't think Sheffield would have taken me back. I had offers from other teams but I didn't want to get on that circuit, having basketball as a number one priority when the financial rewards are not that great can be difficult. It isn't that great an existence.

It wasn't an easy decision. There were all the emotions tangled up with making that decision because I still love the game. Being pragmatic, looking at the financial, long-term picture, it was easy in that sense. If I wasn't being pragmatic, what would I do for a living? I'd rather be playing basketball, in a perfect world, but with basketball being what it is in this country I thought long and hard and came down on the side of career.

I'm delighted with what it's done for the game, pushing stuff forwards. There are two schools of thought. One that bringing more Americans in reduces the opportunities for English kids to play. The school I subscribe to is that the difference they have made to our product has made so many more people interested, made more people pick up a basketball. The whole thing balances itself out.

There are that many people watching on TV, playing in the street, watching games and I would say the product is between one-third and one-half better this year than it has been in previous seasons, particularly in the way it has become so much more competitive.

If you look at teams that are competitive, like Chester. They have been trying to attract the players for years, they have had the money but haven't been able to compete with some of the so-called bigger clubs. This year, they have been able to do that and the result is they have become one of the country's best teams. That explains why we entered the last couple of weeks of the season with five teams in competition for first place.

We would love to welcome back the British players who are abroad, we'd do that tomorrow and reduce the Americans but the fact is that at the moment the British game is not at the level where we can bring them back. We couldn't offer them the money they can get overseas, without bankrupting the sport.

But the challenge for us is to bring the sport up to the level where we can compete with the rest of Europe to bring our higher echelon of player back here. At the rate the game is developing, that may only be a couple of years away.

O McDonald's in Moscow

The World of Basketball

Greece certainly has the most money and prestige of any league in the world, other than the NBA of course. Actually, in some cases there is as much money as the NBA. My team's wage bill this year was $21 million, including the coach.

And the intense fan support is something you have to see to believe. I have been used to English football fans, don't forget, but these supporters are fanatics - in the real sense of the word. They live or die according to how their team does, they are really wild.

Have you seen the movie *The Fan?* Well, that's what fans in Greece are like. They are fans in the literal sense of the word - fanatics.

A fan is somebody who boos and cheers at games, is happy when his team wins and sad when his team loses. A fanatic is different. He lives and dies with the team's fortunes. The perspective is different.

You can be driving down the street and a host of kids can hurl verbal abuse at you because they support the other team in Athens. And, as I'm fond of saying, I wish our uniforms had pockets in their shorts, I'd have made a small fortune this season from all the coins that have been thrown at me. It helps not to be able to speak the language, actually, but you can still tell when someone is yelling at you - whatever the language.

It's quite disappointing really. People there honestly believe they own you. People come and sit next to me in restaurants and tell me, 'I have the right to bother you and talk to you because I buy season tickets.'

I think it's terrible for people to believe they own you. I understand they pay money to watch

basketball and I practice hard so I can entertain them but that's as far as the relationship goes.

The president of one of the regional fan clubs was allowed to address the team one day which struck me as odd. But first he pointed at me and said, 'I want to address you.'

Just before this meeting, one of our team had been hit in the eye by a coin that some idiot had thrown at one of our games and I had come out and said that this was dangerous and unacceptable. Is it worth ruining a guy's career or worse just because he is wearing a different coloured jersey?

So this guy stood up and said to me: 'I hear you think you are in danger by the throwing of coins. Well, that is right, and it is going to get worse if you don't just play!' Incredible.

The year Maccabi played at the Crystal Palace tournament you weren't allowed into the same hotel as them and you were searched going into all the games.

There was more trouble in the Middle East at the time so you weren't allowed anywhere near the players, you were completely segregated from them. At the end of tournament 'do', if you were dancing anywhere near their tables, some big security man would come and guide you away from them.

Moscow has changed beyond all recognition in the years I've been going over there to play. I started going in the days when Marlboros were the most valuable currency and two packets would get you anything, I shudder to think what a pair of Levis was worth back then.

We went to the first Moscow McDonald's, near Red Square, and there must have been a queue of 2,000 Russians out of the door and round the block. We slipped the KGB guy who was assigned to us a couple of packs and we pushed straight in at the front.

There were 18 of us in the party and we all had a full meal, burger, fries, drink, dessert and the bill came to something like 640 roubles. In those days the exchange rate was one rouble to the dollar so we were looking at a $640 bill. We queried this, so the KGB guy gestured: 'Leave it to me.'

He came back a couple of minutes later and asked if anyone had a $20 bill, so one of us gave him it and he said 'OK, that will do!' They were so desperate for the hard currency.

Things have improved a lot for travellers but I still don't see happy people when I go to Moscow. At least under the old regime everybody had work and some sort of food and living - not any more. There is no hope there.

The food is still questionable, as well - apart from McDonald's! Most of the guys take their own food now and on my last trip, one of the players, Karl Brown, went armed with a suitcase full of Pot Noodles. Mind you, Karl is the sort of guy who takes Pot Noodles with him for a road trip to Newcastle!

We played Saratov last season and I swear they were the first Russian team I have ever played who haven't tried to sell us caviar! Every other time a Russian team has come over here they have come armed with pounds of the stuff.

I remember the first time I saw it. They were in with our guys offering them caviar. I said to the Russians 'Look, I've got nine black guys in the team and none of them are Sammy Davis Junior! What do they want with caviar? They wouldn't even know what to do with it!'

Culturally, Switzerland is incredibly different to the States or England. It's just a different world altogether. But basketball is basketball, wherever you go. You're not going to get the black athletes in Switzerland that you get here but you're going to get maybe smarter and more fundamentally sound players, European-style players.

There are different styles wherever you go, here it's much more like the American college game. In Switzerland it's definitely more European, three-point shooting, different systems, stuff like that.

🏀 It was a surprise to find when I got over here that there was no women's team attached to the club. I played for 13 years in Switzerland, starting when I was 11 and won five championships and five cups with Bellinzona.

When I started, there was no women's team, we were among a new intake of female players. We started the whole thing and went on to become the strongest team in Switzerland.

It was really nice that four or five of the players that started at the same time as me got to the top, we built the whole thing up together. It wasn't that we were athletically great or great players but we just had this hope, ambition to win a championship, it brought us together.

But there is nothing here to compare with that system. Joe has two daughters, aged nine and 14, and they really want to play basketball but we find it hard here. In Switzerland it was easy, after school there were so many activities, not just basketball.

🏀 After college I stopped playing for a year, it was a relief really because in my final two years at Long Beach the coach and me had a character conflict and by the end I was just glad to get out of there, it was a weight off my shoulders.

I got the opportunity to play in New Zealand and even though I had a pretty good job, I decided to give it a shot just to see what I could do. It was the best thing that ever happened to me.

I loved New Zealand, it's the third best place in the world after Samoa and England. England is great because the people speak English. You wouldn't believe the difference that makes to your life, especially after I played in Taiwan and Hong Kong.

Personally, I didn't enjoy my time over there. I found that the Chinese people were a bit stand-offish with certain other people. If you weren't English, I mean white and from England rather than English-speaking, they would treat you like a peasant.

I stayed in one of the richest areas of Hong Kong and it was horrible. You really need to have plenty of money to have any kind of life there, there is so much squalor.

The one thing about playing in New Zealand was it allowed me to start going to Samoa. I was actually born in the States but my parents are Samoan and, as far as I'm concerned, I AM Samoan.

I've been playing for the national team since '87 and been going there every summer since '92 for camps and clinics. It was great in New Zealand because it's only a one hour 45 minute flight away and there are probably more Samoan people in New Zealand than there are in Samoa itself. That's the one problem with England - too far from Samoa.

🏀 The first thing that struck me about coming to Newcastle was that it is an excellent organisation, first class, man.

I spent last season in Israel and that was a real culture shock for someone like me, arriving from America. Their Prime Minister was shot while I was there and there were explosions. I couldn't wait to get home once the season was over with.

Basketball wise, there is some good talent over there, no doubt about it. But the facilities are not as professional as they are in England. The arenas in Israel can't compare with those I'm playing in now. Newcastle's venue is also a lot better than the CBA arena I played in earlier this season.

I was with the Florida Beachdogs, about an hour from Miami. It was beautiful down there but I'd played five or six games when the Newcastle opportunity came up and I jumped at it. The fans have been great and every game I've played in

has been really competitive, and most have gone down to the wire. I'm really enjoying it.

🕐 We had heard of Chester before we got the offer. Playing in Ireland, we had kept up with English basketball through the magazines and Sky TV coverage. It looked attractive. We knew about the big arenas and the format of the season was a lot better with more games and when we heard about the four American rule we knew the competition would definitely be better.

For me, Chester and Ireland are kind of the same. You know, a laid back lifestyle compared to where I'm from - New York City.

The main difference I've noticed in coming over to England is in the population. There are a lot more people here than there were in Ireland, more variety of nationalities, stuff like that. When we were in Ireland, there just weren't that many black guys.

It was hard when we first went to Ireland, it was such a big difference. Luckily, one of my team mates Ricardo Leonard is from Washington DC so I had someone I could relate to and that made it that much easier for me. Plus, we had basketball games every week which gave you something to focus on so I fitted in pretty comfortably.

People think, 'Oh, you're from New York City, it must be real boring here.' Yes, it definitely is quiet here but I'm a quiet guy. I enjoy the peaceful lifestyle of getting prepared for the game, just relaxing, taking it easy.

○ You might not like basketball, but you want to beat the French

England in Europe

🕐 The English game is more athletic than in Europe, although I think players over there tend to be bigger. I'm not one of your more athletic players so moving here from Germany took some getting used to.

I think there is more concentration on defence over there and players tend to have better fundamentals, much better three-point shooting, for example.

But for speed and athleticism, English basketball, and English players are on a par with the rest of Europe, if not better. The game seems very fast here as opposed to Germany where it was slower, more deliberate.

🕐 The League probably aren't bothered about one of their teams doing well in Europe but what they don't realise is that for our game to be taken as a serious product in Britain, the sporting public will want to see us doing well against the rest of the continent.

Somebody, either the national team or a club team, has got to stand up and make the public appreciate that this is a serious product we have now. Until then, it doesn't matter how great our own domestic league is. We have to step outside that and show what we can do against the rest of the world.

European competition gets people off the fence, you see that in soccer. You're going against the French, you might not like basketball, but you certainly want to beat the French! And the Germans, and the Spanish. That gets people, even neutrals, interested and behind you.

That's why the only thing left for me to achieve in

coaching is success in Europe. For most coaches in England their goal is to win in England and that's great. Don't get me wrong, I still hate losing games in England. But my goal is a whole lot higher. I like being successful at home, but if you're successful in Europe I believe the domestic business takes care of itself.

That is one of the reasons I feel we have to change the rule of allowing English teams to use five foreigners, when you can only use two in European competition. As long as that rule exists, I can't see any English team being successful in Europe.

🏀 Coaches here have to adapt themselves more to the European style of basketball. The closest thing to us culturally is the States so it should be no surprise the kids want to play that way. The problem is not with the kids, it's with the coaches who have to be able to teach them a more European approach.

Until they do that as a country - be it club or national team - we are not going to compete with Europe, not until we switch to their style of basketball.

Because our kids are athletically like the States, if we can mix that ability with European strategies, technique, tactics, it would be a potent mixture. You would have a different type of player to the one we currently produce, but hopefully better teams who are athletically superior to the rest of Europe and playing the way they need to compete in Europe.

This all stems from how the kids are taught and the fact we have so many American players in here who are playing an American college style of game. In contrast, you look at French and German teams. They have two Americans and the rest are European players. Germans are playing in Greece, French players in Italy because they've all been brought up playing a very similar style of basketball.

The sad thing is, other people have not recognised this, or they have recognised it and not done anything about it.

overtime

" if you're not going to compete,
then I'll dominate you "

michael jordan

White men can jump

Racism

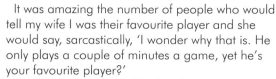

🎤 Among players I've never seen examples of racism, I really can't think of an example. I've seen it from the crowd, I'm sad to say. You know, taunts and jibes from the crowd, especially around five or six years ago when I was playing in Birmingham.

Of course, it's easy for me to say that because I'm white. If you asked black players, they might find things racist that I don't perceive that way. But, to me, your team mates are among your best friends, whatever their colour.

I think it is something you also see more of at junior levels. Perhaps by the time players get to senior level they have been used to playing against the same guys for years and that helps remove racism.

But I could imagine Manchester's junior team, for example, who are probably 85 per cent black, having problems when they go somewhere like Shropshire, where I was brought up, where nine of the junior team are probably white.

As far as top level basketball was concerned, if a guy got a reputation as a racist I don't think he would last long in this league. He would have the proverbial kicked out of him. He'd get an elbow from every black player in the league.

To me, if you are a racist person I don't think you would have been attracted to basketball in the first place, it is such a mixed, multi-cultural sport. That's one of the most attractive things about the game.

🎤 At one point last season I was the only white guy on the team, now there are none. I was never really made aware or uncomfortable of the fact from the players, but I was from supporters.

It was amazing the number of people who would tell my wife I was their favourite player and she would say, sarcastically, 'I wonder why that is. He only plays a couple of minutes a game, yet he's your favourite player?'

The black players would joke about it to me but not in any threatening or upsetting way. I'd hear the old thing about white guys not being able to jump and if I dunked it they would all pretend to be surprised - 'Oh, white men CAN jump.'

🎤 I think we have one black kid in our club, at under 19, he's probably the first we've had. There just isn't a big black population in Barrow.

You hear the common conception that blacks make more athletic basketball players than whites - you know, the 'white men can't jump' syndrome. I don't think race is an issue, I just think that historically and culturally, the sport has been seen as a black sport.

You can trace it back to the States and the Harlem Globetrotter-style exhibition teams and, of course, the fact that the majority of players in the NBA now are black.

A lot of kids think it's a black sport and I think in this country black kids feel it's their game and basketball has consequently attracted more of them. I don't think they're any more particularly athletic than white kids, I just think that more black youngsters are attracted to the sport.

I think that is to the sport's credit. Black youngsters see basketball as offering them more opportunities than rugby or even football. As a consequence, I think you are going to see more athletic blacks in the game than athletic whites.

🎤 I was one of the first white players they could get to go to my university. It was an all-black team for many years. I think I was the first white scholarship player to play in about five years.

Back then there was still a lot of racial unrest on campus and a lot of things going on generally.

Some guys on my team were involved in taking over the students' union. There was certainly some militancy in the air.

There was a black fraternity on campus and they weren't allowed to talk to me on campus during the day while they were doing their pledge, which lasted for 30 days. I had team mates and they told me they intended no disrespect and we would be all hunky-dory in the locker-room, but they couldn't talk to me anywhere else.

It was really wild back then and I got phone calls from people - some anonymous - telling me not to go there and play on a black team, telling me I wouldn't be happy or saying that people would do things to me, threats which were a bunch of rubbish. But it was a tough time for me.

The racial issue didn't make any difference to me because I grew up playing in the parks and already knew a couple of guys, black guys, on the university team. One of them, Tony Hansen who is actually living in England now but was originally from Jamaica and went on to be an All-American, called me and said he really wanted me to play on the team.

There were a couple of small incidents when I first got there, but after I showed that it didn't bother me, that was over, and I loved my college career.

Coming from Hartford, where the team played, they actually had a Joe Whelton day in my honour! I was guest at the state capitol, there was the Governor of the state shaking the hand of this little white kid.

🏀 I really don't think racism is an issue in basketball in this country in the same way that it has been in the States. Basketball has been adopted in Britain as, if not a black sport, then a sport that a lot of black people play.

In America it was different. For social reasons, it was a whites only sport and became gradually integrated over the years. Here the sport started on an equal footing in racial terms. You look at the

number of black coaches in the British game, compared to how long the League has been going, and it is quite a high figure. Look at the NBA in the States and they are crying out for black people to be given jobs in coaching and management.

Here, we have a healthy situation where a black guy like Mike Shaft is the main commentator of the sport on a major network. That sort of situation does not exist in the States.

The only thing I would point to here is that I don't see many blacks in management positions, whether at clubs, or the EBBA or the League itself. I don't know if that's by chance or whether no-one applies but the fact is the League must be made up of at least 80 per cent black players, yet no blacks are in those positions. We need to focus on getting all cultures involved at all levels.

Personally, I have never experienced racial abuse in this country, for the reasons I have outlined above. It wouldn't make any difference, after some of the things I've experienced in the States I would be able to rise above it easily.

The only time I have been aware of racial comments is when we were playing the Leopards and I called Robert Youngblood a 'black ***!' The ref said if there was any more racial abuse he would throw me out of the game. I said, 'Wait a minute, how is that racial abuse? I'm black as well, you know!'

O Worrying about making the minimum wage

O **Drugs in Basketball**

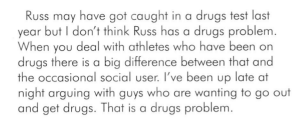

It was with sadness that I heard of Russ Saunders' suspension from the game for taking an illegal drug. He was the first player to catch my eye back in '81. I wondered how this little man could race from one end of the court to the other in between the 'trees' and score at will.

Basketball had always intrigued me but it wasn't until I went to comprehensive school in Birmingham and gained encouragement from Dick Jones, the head of PE, that I began to play and learned to love the sport.

Dick arranged for Russ to give a clinic at school and his ball-handling took the breath away. I suppose, as a youngster, your tendency is to gaze at the playmaker, rather than other positions. Just as kids playing football on a park want to be Alan Shearer rather than a defender.

And when it came to play-making, Russ was the best. What he does now with his life remains to be seen, but I'll always remember and appreciate him for the great player he was.

When I was at college, you faced NCAA tests at tournaments and the school made you take tests. There were three things you didn't mess with at our school - drugs, missing classes and turnovers! Turnovers would probably actually be first on that list.

But a friend of mine got in trouble over a drugs test and had to go to rehab. He had me do an internship at the rehab centre with him and I worked with this group of athletes who were in there. I was real fortunate to be able to work closely with them and see exactly what a drug problem is.

Russ may have got caught in a drugs test last year but I don't think Russ has a drugs problem. When you deal with athletes who have been on drugs there is a big difference between that and the occasional social user. I've been up late at night arguing with guys who are wanting to go out and get drugs. That is a drugs problem.

Perhaps the story that best illustrates my attitude to basketball - and why I didn't progress to the level people felt I should have - came when I was younger, before a national college final when I was at Stockport College. We had played five games and won them all by at least 20 points and the night before the final, a few of us - I could name names, but I won't - went out and got completely sloshed.

In the final, we lost to the worst team, Northampton I think it was, by some margin. The moral of the story? Don't get sloshed the night before a big game.

But it was times like that, when other things got in the way of my basketball - my belly, for instance - that I realised I might not be able to make it as a top class player.

We take the drugs issue very seriously but I don't really see it being a big problem in our game right now. I'm not being blasé, it's just that there is not enough money being made. When players are making $200-300,000 a year then you might have a problem, when they have that much money to go out and party with.

Most American guys right now are more worried about making the minimum wage, which is more like £300 a week. And English players are not dealing with drugs, most of them are worrying about holding down a second job. You can start off being a casual drug user but eventually it is going to take hold of you and soon you are going to start putting both jobs at risk.

It's only when you have too much money and

time on your hands that this is going to become a major issue here.

 After an England game in Newcastle, Roger Huggins was picked out for a drugs test and, as is so often the case in these things, he couldn't 'go' straight away after the game.

I was driving him back to Sheffield so I had to wait as well and we must have been there for an hour and a half, forcing water and soft drinks down him until he finally gave a sample.

We eventually set off back to Sheffield and, of course, the inevitable happened, we had to stop at four successive service stations between Scotch Corner and Wetherby so that Roger could relieve himself!

 I don't think drugs is a big issue any more, the players get tested so often, although having said that, you still hear stories and rumours occasionally.

But this was in the eighties when it was a totally different story, drugs were rife. Larry Dacey, whose dead now sadly - he got killed in a car accident - was playing for the Hemel team and Fred, my husband, went into their dressing room after the game, as he usually does, to see that everything was alright.

Larry was in there with another player, who better remain nameless, and Fred came back up to where we were in the bar and told us their dressing room atmosphere had been thick with smoke. He said they had kept offering him this cigarette they were passing round and in the end he had to come out to get some fresh air.

Fred kept chattering away and just wouldn't shut up and in the end we had to tell him that the cigarette they had been passing around was dope! He said that it had smelt funny but Fred was as high as a kite for hours, that's how naive he is, though.

O Establishing itself in the spectator marketplace

Big Business

 I was chatting to Mike Burton about where the game is at now and he said he was sat around the table at the last league meeting and counted six or seven millionaires sat there with him. That's when he realised that basketball has now arrived.

Chris Wright, Ed Simons, Harvey Goldsmith, these are all people who have made it in their own right, in their own field, and they are not going to do bad deals. People like them, and Sir John Hall, will be in it for the ride.

Everybody is looking at pro basketball now as a sound business investment. It won't be long before somebody floats on the stock market, and it won't be long before more people follow Newcastle's example and go for the sports club setup. Sheffield United and Leeds United football clubs are looking at it. They are making a huge investment for the future and we've never had that before. It all points to a solid future at the top for the sport and there are lots of good things happening at the bottom of the sport.

 It's been good to last 15 years in this league, good to have the chance to see a lot of changes, see the game flourish, then fall back, then restart all over again. It's been like a phoenix, burning up and coming back again.

There are still problems and concerns and it's still frustrating to me to know that there is talent coming from England now but people have to look to go and play in Europe to make real money because the wages just aren't here. I really believe that's the key issue in the game that has to be considered.

We have players, kids, going off to the States to improve their game but when they come back what

incentive is there to stay and play in England when you have to play basketball and take an extra job to make ends meet. You end up doing two jobs, not one. How can I fulfil my potential as a basketball player if I'm having to hold down two jobs? And all because wages here are repressed by a salary cap.

Don't get me wrong. A lot of players have been fortunate to have good employers over the years who have let them have time off for games and training. But generally we are still more amateur than professional and, of course, when we go and play in Europe, we're playing teams who are fully pro. We might be going against a team whose budget is $4 million and ours might be a fraction of that. The opposition will have one player making more than our whole budget!

It doesn't feel right when guys can go and play in the lower divisions in Europe and make more money than they can at home. That is something that has to be addressed.

The cap is ridiculous and it has to go. Not only is it ridiculously low but it also includes the coaches' and team managers' salaries. I don't think the idea of our league should be to reward those teams who aren't going to invest in the game and in talent. I believe you have to speculate to accumulate in business. And sports is business.

🏀 Where will we be five years from now? Obviously we have been able to attract some very high profile owners, been able to move to new arenas. I see us moving to a mix of owner-arenas, facilities owned by the club themselves - such as the plan Mike Horton has in Derby - and the bigger arenas as they come on stream.

And I see the sport as having established itself in the spectator market place with the game being complemented by lots of kids playing it in the outdoor initiative and other situations. Really, I would say I would see it as having a raised profile, more of the same, establishing where we are.

The coverage on Sky has been brilliant in terms of establishing and creating an excitement for the product we currently have. Every season since I've been with the League there has been a point where you think we cannot possibly top that, great games or high-point events when you think, 'Can we ever top that?' But we always have. You think that, then you get a season like the last one which in terms of quality of games and excitement has been brilliant.

🏀 When I was appointed we had a five year business plan and I've been very much involved in the implementation of that. The plan, put simply, was to create franchises and become a media-driven sport.

The only people that rang me when I first came here were people asking me for money. Now, maybe 70 per cent of our calls are media phone calls. People ring us now as distinct from us calling them. Of six full-time staff, maybe four are dealing with the media.

We are dealing with creating an image, sales, attitude, supporting the clubs as they establish successful franchises. We have adapted that five year plan, moved it on. We feel that from the initial approach, we now have a lot more to achieve, that's why the plan is evolving, revised all the time.

I've been very pleased with the progress and the plan, which has made us focus on what are the important issues.

🏀 I think the immediate appeal of the sport to a company like ours lies in the comparison to where basketball was ten, even five, years ago.

We feel this is just the first step in many steps the game can take in this country. Ten years ago, when it was taking its first tentative steps in this country, there was no real belief. There was no structure, finance, resources, facilities in place or money with the ownership. We never felt, for example, that the sport would go anywhere other than the stage it had already reached.

People in basketball would approach us with proposals and we would say, 'Yes, fine, but we will talk to you in five years time and the picture will be exactly the same.'

Now you look at its current state and you have got to invest in it. It is going to roll on, Channel 4, the NBA, the whole picture is only going to grow.

We will always be number one because of our global position but now with the potential in the UK market, it would be good to be number one here in basketball. To me, that means being a little bit creative, in terms of grass roots stuff, coaching, participation, rather than going out and buying up kit rights to all the top teams in the country.

To give you an idea, our company budget in basketball has increased 100 fold over the past four years and we're one of the major players, revenue-wise, which is good because I'd always been the strongest advocate that we didn't need to do anything in basketball, the sport was not worth getting involved in, it was so local, so small, no big sponsors.

Of course, the youth market is vital to all this. Our brand is a very young brand and sometimes we try to temper that by directing activity to the older consumer. We try to keep it at the 11-25 group, right in there with the profile of the sport.

We're also very aware that basketball is a girls' sport - not girls' fitness, a SPORT. That women's fitness thing is very passé now. I think women are almost offended if you say to them, 'Oh, you're into women's fitness.' They come back and say, 'No, I play women's sport.'

Basketball is not quite the equal split that tennis gives you but basketball gives you the opportunity to involve girls, it gives you that girl participation, a girl fan base.

Right now, basketball footwear doesn't really sell. It's running and outdoor stuff. But the pendulum of fashion could well come back to basketball and, in 12-18 months time, you could see every kid on the street wearing them. Right now, it's the urban city culture look, the shoes, the over-sized jackets image. But the good thing is that our efforts to get the kids playing are not going to be effected by fads and fashion.

🏀 I'd say my commitment here, both as an organisation and personally, is very strong. I know my partners and organisation are committed here and we won't be walking away. We're here and one way or another we will be here for a long long time.

I don't worry about success, I worry more about have we put on a great night, have we looked after our sponsors, have the fans that have been there had a terrific night? Yes I walk away from there feeling a lot better if we have won, but if we've given them the best night's entertainment that we can then they will come back. But you don't have to win everything, you can still sell out without winning.

🏀 Professional basketball is like a new sport these days, a lot stronger compared to some of the times I have known over the last 15 years.

The actual game is a lot stronger because of the input of more Americans but not only that, basketball is more professional, more full-time than in the past. More clubs are now trying to take it to the next level whereas in the past I think clubs were almost trying not to let it take off.

Now there is a big influx of big clubs and big owners with big money behind them. There are great things going on in Manchester. Sir John Hall is bringing his sporting experience to bear on Newcastle, Derby are building an arena, Birmingham have great things happening and even clubs like Leicester and Chester, who have not traditionally been strong, are building arenas and building for the future.

There is more of an input and investment in the future of the sport and that is why I am optimistic about the direction in which it is heading.

Basketball's got a shot at really making it as a major sport in the UK. It's a major sport in a lot of countries in the world and it's got a real possibility to make it a big sport here.

We looked at several sports, ice hockey first and then basketball and basketball appealed to me more, for the scene of it, the fashion, the clothing. It was happening and it IS happening with the young people in our society now.

America's taught us a lot, and so has the rest of the world, about entertaining people and how sport has changed the way it's presented now, whereby you have a complete entertainment package for people.

Am I making money? Well, I'm losing less this year than last year. In round numbers, for me to stage a basketball tournament at Wembley Arena costs me around £18-20,000. That much. That's without advertising, paying people, it's a lot of money.

People compare basketball to football whereas, in my mind, we are talking about very different sports. Football had to start somewhere and now it is reaping the benefits in terms of investors, sponsors and the potential there is for players to become involved in that side of things.

You look at us and yes, we're at an early stage. But if you look at who's getting involved with it, look at the amount Nike and Adidas are investing in English basketball, and it tells you something.

The NBA, also. I think they have their own agenda set for the UK, but they have triggered off people like Nike becoming more active. It's great that the NBA are doing their road shows and tours and getting the media coverage. In an ideal world, we would like to work hand in hand and help each other, I just don't know enough to know whether that would be possible.

Walking into the Nynex in Manchester for the first time, I looked around and thought, 'This is

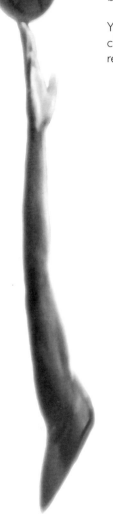

what it's all about.' The atmosphere, the presentation, the actual vastness of it, made you feel part of something very big, very special.

In the past, basketball traditionally went to leisure centres. It was all okay but let's face it, it just wasn't glamorous. It's a bit 'hockey sticks and cricket bats,' it's not an event, a night-out like basketball is today.

It's a sport, but it's also an entertainment event. You go in, get the music, get the mascots, the cheerleaders, the PA, you feel part of something really special.

Frederick, you are not going to Newcastle

Moving Teams

My feeling was one of absolute despondency when Doncaster folded. We had been involved for 22 years although for the last year we were not so heavily involved and my husband Fred didn't manage the team.

My heart wasn't really in it for that last year, everything had changed and the whole thing had stopped being friendly. The council decided they weren't happy with the way the Dome was running it and charged us £21,500 for the season - that, when our total sponsorship package was £43,000! And that was before wages or court hire for practice was added.

In Doncaster, there are only three potential sponsors and none of them were interested, although it looked as though Caspian might take us over when they bought Leeds United Football Club. They approached us with a view to keeping us there for two years then moving to Leeds but that didn't work out either.

After that, I put my foot down and told Fred we were finished with basketball. Of course, that lasted all of four weeks until Ken Nottage called us and asked if Fred wanted to get involved as team manager.

Well, I put my foot down and said 'Frederick, you're not going to Newcastle.' But we went up there to have a look and then someone said the magic words to me - 'We will pay you for doing the washing.'

That was the first time in 22 years that someone had made that offer to me and that was it, I was sold on the idea.

I'm 68 and Fred's retiring in March at 65 and, after Doncaster, I never thought we'd find another club or have any real interest in basketball again. It was like losing a close friend when the Panthers folded. But being at Newcastle is like being part of a big family again. They can't do enough for you.

Now we've got our great nephew involved and all the cupboard space that I thought I was going to get back has gone again. It's full of uniforms and equipment. And I've had to forget about all the odd-jobs around the house that Fred was going to do for me in his spare time. And I couldn't be happier.

This whole business of taking over a club lock, stock and barrel is alien to us. I know that it happens all the time in the States. A team that has been in one city for 20 years will move overnight hundreds, if not thousands, of miles.

That's unheard of here. Remember a few years ago when Luton Town football team talked of moving to Milton Keynes? There was a huge outcry and that's just a few miles we're talking about.

There was a bit of an outcry when Sunderland moved to Newcastle a couple of years ago, especially with what had happened with the Durham Wasps ice hockey team. They were bought by Newcastle Sporting Club and there was a lot of acrimony, even legal moves, over them going to Newcastle. Eventually, Durham Ice Rink ended up closing because of the loss of revenue.

There was slightly less fuss about the basketball team but, even so, the Sunderland Echo was full of anti-John Hall letters, 'Who's he think he is, buying up our team?'

My two kids have just started to go to watch Newcastle this season. Last year they went, but only under sufferance. My wife says I have them brainwashed, they hate Newcastle United football team and don't want to have anything to do with the basketball because of it.

They used to go to watch Sunderland basketball at Washington or Crowtree all the time. Then the

team came to Newcastle and they were very reticent. Last season I had to convince them they were nothing to do with the football club and I got them to go to a few matches, but they still weren't sure. Then once the basketball team actually became Newcastle United they refused to go.

It actually became embarrassing at Christmas when Sir John Hall threw a party for all the staff of the Sporting Club, everyone from the football, rugby, ice hockey, basketball.

It was at St James' Park, a real lavish do with no expense spared, beautiful food and extravagant gifts for the kids. There were about 160 kids in total but very few of the basketball team have got children so Diane was under pressure to fly the flag and take ours.

I got out of having to go because I had work so my mum, who knows Sir John Hall and his wife from way back, went instead ... and they said they have never been as embarrassed in their lives!

The kids sat there sulking, refusing to join in with any of the games, they wouldn't eat, wouldn't talk to anyone. At one stage, Sir John's wife came over and asked what the problem was and my mum had to explain the whole situation. She tried to explain that this wasn't really a football team 'do' but the kids weren't having any of it. The only time they cheered up slightly was when their names were read out and they were given their presents. As soon as they left St James', they cheered up.

My wife and mother blame me and say I've indoctrinated them but I say they've just got strong minds of their own! But I do admit I refuse to go to St James' unless Sunderland are playing there. I only broke that once and that was earlier this season when there was another Sporting Club 'do' ... where there was £10 free drink for everyone. So, I reluctantly went, especially when Tom Hancock - who doesn't drink - gave me his £10 worth as well.

○ Ten thousand goals

Development Issues

🏀 I say to people that if you look at the history of anything that has succeeded, it has never been the career person that has caused something to happen, it has always been the enthusiast, the person who has put their heart into it, that has got things rolling, made things happen.

I've always believed, and still do, that it is enthusiasm that will take a sport forward. I always argue that when people are being put in posts, for example as development officers, that these people should have basketball backgrounds. They are going to create more and more interest in the game if they have that passion for it, rather than someone who is just in the job because it is a career move. They might do a good job, but you need that desire, that enthusiasm for a sport.

🏀 We tend to find that kids play most sports and the good ones tend to be good at all sports and they're all wanted by the football, rugby, basketball teams. By the time they reach year ten some begin making decisions which way they are going to go.

We take some from other sports, as they do from us. At the moment I have 33 kids in year seven in my own school but by the time they get to year nine or ten that will be down to 15 but they will be 15 out and out basketball players. Playing-wise the sport is absolutely taking off at the moment. When we first became involved we weren't doing too well. Our catchment area in Barrow was a lot smaller and it was difficult to break through or do anything on a national level. You might have the odd team that would come through but, since the club expanded and our catchment area got bigger we've taken off.

What we've noticed, though, is that even though all this has happened, we've found it harder than ever to get right to the top, to the top two or three in the country which is what we have done in the past. It shows how the standard generally is getting so much better.

Four or five years ago we were at the finals every single year, the last couple of years we've not quite got there, basically because teams are coming through from other areas, particularly those where there are Bud League teams setting up clinics and development.

We have to rely on pure and simple team work, we don't get the good athletic kids that other clubs get. You've got to work on keeping the kids a long while, drilling them and drilling them until they become good team players. Other big city teams are getting the big athletic kids that might have gone into football or rugby in years gone by.

We are still slowly improving, it's just that other clubs are getting better quicker and attracting better players into the game.

● I had the deputy head give me the big talk when I told school I was going to stop playing rugby, and then when I made the England under-17 and under-19 teams they wanted to put me in the local papers!

They wanted to boost the school's image so I said no. When I needed help, you know time I could spend in the gym practising, they said no. I think that sort of problem still goes on at some schools.

I was quite good at rugby and they wanted me to go for trials, they figured I could make the South-West team at under-18 but my brother Joe was playing basketball, I used to go and watch him and gradually got into it.

Squash and rugby were my sports at the time but basketball just took over. It was more fun as a sport and I enjoyed the people more. The basketball people I was around didn't care where you were from or what you did, they were just there to have fun. You could hang out with them and feel at ease whereas you couldn't with the rugby crowds, especially as you got older.

There were more cliques in rugby, more of the old boy network. It was too much for me to take. You had to be in with the in-crowd, whereas basketball people just accepted you for what you were, they never tried to change you. In rugby, if you didn't go to the pub, didn't get blind drunk, you weren't a rugby boy.

● There was no basketball team at Stockport Grammar School when I was there, so I started one. Now it's something they're quite proud of. It wasn't very high profile then, but now they have kids playing for English Schools.

It's interesting because at the time they were really mad with me for giving up rugby to play basketball. I remember the head teacher telling me I would never make anything of myself in basketball.

Now I go back and I'm given the red carpet, hero's homecoming treatment.

● I've been working in the department of recreation at home ever since I was 14. I started basketball late, at 15, which is real late for an American.

I've taught kids in America who are seven or eight who have pretty good fundamental skills. That's just because where we're from that's what you play. You play basketball, football, baseball, depending on the season. Most athletes in the States will have grown up playing at least two of them real seriously.

When I go back in summer to clinics I've seen ten-year-old kids who dribble the ball better than me! They can do things with the ball that I can't do, behind the back dribbles, spin moves … it's fun to watch them growing up and improving every year.

It's frustrating, then, when you go to a camp here sometimes and ask a 15 or 16-year-old group to start lay-up lanes and they can't even do that, or dribble the ball right-hand left-hand up and down court.

You have to be patient and teach them how to do the basics, then you go home, step onto court, throw the ball in the air and they run a lay-up line straight away.

It's just an education issue. At home, everywhere you go there are kids playing basketball, indoor, outdoor, whatever the season.

I think it's moving up here but until guys get to the point where they want to play the game from a very early age then you've still got a long way to go. But the good thing is there are kids in England now who are living and eating basketball. I've seen improvements in the four years I've been in Europe but you have to know it's a slow process.

🏀 The thing about high school in the States is that if you are struggling academically there are teachers who will give you As to make sure you can still keep playing on the basketball team.

You pick all the easy classes to start with - sports fashion or sports marketing, for example - and I've still known teachers who have told players, 'Just sit there and keep quiet and I'll give you an A!' It's amazing, and wrong.

🏀 High school in the States was definitely a culture shock. You look around, you see a lack of discipline you don't see in English schools, but there is a lot more friendliness, teachers are supposed to be more your friend and mentor than your teacher.

There is a combination of sports and school spirit, which aren't a priority in English schools. Yes, you might get your parents coming to watch you play rugby games but in the States we would get 3,000 people at a high school basketball match! The whole school and the community at large would come out. It's a home product, something they can support and relate to. It was something and somebody they saw every day and to them the NBA is just not the same as seeing Joe Smith from down the road score a touchdown or shoot a three.

We had to go to the University of Toledo, which holds 10,000, for games and sometimes we would have crowds of 6-7,000. It was ridiculous! It blew my mind but it was a very rewarding experience.

And that is something that maybe holds together some high schools in the worst areas of inner-city America. In the midst of problems with drugs, crime, issues about family, in the midst of that, communities are held together by school sport.

🏀 I remember a time when school sports was football, rugby, if there was a third sport, it might be basketball but then only if the school had a court and the time to do it. Now in the Wakefield area, where I'm involved, the majority of schools would fail to raise a full rugby team. It's football and basketball in that order.

That's perhaps surprising in Yorkshire which you might expect to be one of the country's more traditional, conservative - with a small 'c' - areas. But it is fashionable and I think it is a game where anybody, at any level, can play.

I take a team at year eight, the 13-14 level, and at that age I find that a lot of girls are better than boys, more skilful, maybe more experienced, which the boys don't like. At that level, school basketball is pretty much non-contact so you can play mixed games with no worries, which is another attraction.

I recently read about a girl of that age who wanted to play rugby league and was better than a lot of boys her own age but she couldn't play, for obvious reasons I suppose, but there is never that issue in basketball.

🏀 The Leicester basketball community is growing. They are very knowledgeable fans. We're not

necessarily like Leicester City Football Club who have hundreds of thousands of 'em, but the fans we do have turn up, more than I thought they would, and they are a very knowledgeable crowd.

We go into the schools and the kids are greatly interested in the sport although it still has an image of a 'new' thing. The first thing I did when I walked into my first school here was look at the kids' feet and most of them were wearing soccer shoes.

But that's only the same as if Kasey Keller, the Leicester goalkeeper, were to go into a school in the US where he comes from and talk to kids in a gym. They would all be wearing basketball sneakers. It is a question of what they are most comfortable with and where their hearts lie. I think kids' hearts in this country will always be with football but I think basketball can slowly creep its way in there because the sport seems so intriguing and interesting to kids here.

● For me, Newcastle and Manchester are now the homes of the game in this country, Sheffield and Birmingham also make a nice presentation of the game. But these arenas are the circumstances in which you now have to present a game.

You need a gym where you can really entertain the people, accommodate the people to watch the games in comfort and enjoyment.

When the national team has played at Leicester, the Granby Halls, it is like a barn. Let's face the fact, it is a disgrace for the national team to play there.

These are your own people, your own countrymen, that is why you have to treat them properly and give them nice surroundings in which to watch the game.

It speaks of the team when they play at some state of the art arena rather than somewhere like Granby Halls. Leicester may be a nice arena for some things, but it is not a nice arena for the England national team. People look around and see that it's grimy and wonder why are England playing here?

It's like putting the England football team at Stockport County's ground. I like Stockport's ground but they are not going to play the national football team there.

The game has a whole different feel to it when it is played at a nice arena in front of a big crowd, it sets a tone right from the start of the game. The other important thing is kids playing the game need something to aspire to and they have a higher standard of aspirations if they see their national team playing at a big arena.

● I thought it was significant that when they had posters up in Moss Side, promoting the Hulme development that the one sporting image they chose was basketball. There was a picture of the multi-cultural nuclear family with the little lad wearing a Jordan vest. Not a Manchester City or United shirt, but Bulls number 23. I thought that made a strong commentary on the place that the sport now has in this country - certainly in inner cities.

League clubs. That, I think, is the key thing. Outside of that I believe the best a club can do is work on a break-even policy in generating bums on seats.

What Sky TV have done is present sport in a very dynamic way. Basketball is getting better presented all the time and that is the major issue.

I hope Channel 5 is relatively established in a year, maybe they will want to take it because £3-5 million would be the financial security and status we need. I think we want and warrant somewhere more around £5-10 million, just under half of what they are paying rugby union, but if the lower figure comes in then we are talking about having thirteen £1 million turnover clubs and suddenly everybody is interested in you. Partners, sponsors, everybody. We saw that in Sheffield with the Eagles in rugby league, as soon as Sky came on board, it opened so many doors for them.

There is no doubt that big TV money would help this sport immeasurably, but let's get into the real world. Sky TV aren't going to pay £5 million for it unless they have to and unless a rival is prepared to offer that sort of money, that isn't going to happen.

Premier League football sells their dishes more than anything and buying rugby union was a step towards getting the home nations internationals which, again, would sell dishes. What else would they pay a lot of money for? Bits of golf, cricket, athletics, maybe.

There has to be someone else after it for them to cough up. Let's hope. There are various opportunities with more channels coming on line. I mean, Channel 5 launched with three live baseball matches. What's all that about?

Broadcast opportunities are increasing in so many sports and basketball is a good TV sport. The trick for us is to maintain the product and maintain the interest, keep the audience growing and the coverage growing with it.

We're pleased with the media coverage the sport's now getting. We did a quick analysis in the autumn and it was 100 per cent up on last season which we've got to be very pleased with indeed.

Having said that, we can always have more coverage but that's an issue for the clubs, really, how much emphasis they want to put on it. There is more we could exploit, more we could do but, at the moment, we don't really have the resources to do that.

We're very strong regionally, increasing our strength in the nationals and moving across other media, into radio and TV. People ask when we're going to make the real media breakthrough but we aren't going to suddenly wake up one morning and find it has happened. You've got to keep chip, chip, chipping away.